I0622728

Remember When

Times That Made Me Laugh, Cry,

and Everything in Between

by MARK ALBERTS

ISBN: 979-8-9895632-0-3 (print)
ISBN: 979-8-9895632-1-0 (ebook)

Book Cover by Brandi Avant

First edition 2023

TABLE OF CONTENTS

CHAPTER I

Some First Memories

Remember When...

I can remember things from way back. I don't know if this is common or not, but I can remember times when I was in diapers. OK, granted I was in diapers until age ten and probably will return there soon just for convenience. Seriously, I do remember some things from when I was young.

For example, I remember the time we lived in California. My dad went off to Vietnam when I was two. I do not remember much in between; I just remember him showing back up. Kind of like my older sister, who was just there. I don't remember when I officially recognized her as my older sister, just that one day while sitting in the backyard, playing in the mud created from the air conditioning drain, she decided to put something from a dropper in my eyes. Jimminey Crickets, that burned like hades.

Needless to say, I went blind, and my sister now lives with a guilt complex. She lives homeless in a mansion and has paid me off numerous times. Well, maybe I was not exactly blind. What really happened was, I screamed and cried so loud that the San Bernardino fire department was notified. Thankfully, my mom was a nurse and was able to save my sight and stop the burning. All while saying, "You know you are his sister and should not put anything in your brother's eyes." Right then, I knew I had a sister!

Now my second sister, I found out about her when she was in my mommy's belly. Yep, that is right. I was an intuitive little rascal and at the ripe ole age of four-something, I guessed correctly that I would have a younger sister. In fact, I'd sit and talk to that critter in my mom's belly trying to persuade her not to blind me and beware of our older sister. I felt it was my brotherly duty to give her a heads up (or down) about having a sister.

Anyway, my younger sister was born four years after I arrived and I had, thankfully, learnt a few things prior to her arrival. She and I were close, I felt. My older sister and I were cordial and to be honest I was intimidated by her. She was so smart, very strong, and gorgeous. I couldn't compete with that and really did not try. I just sat back and admired her accomplishments. Do not tell her that I have said that, because she did blind me once in my life, remember.

So, my younger sister and I were generally good buddies from the get-go. She also is gorgeous and strong. She is smart too, but anyone sitting in a room with our older sister would not seem that bright. In fact, I think even ole Albert E. would fade into the background. My younger sister and I would hang out and I would sing to her or tell her stupid things. Well, that lasted pretty much until I left the house.

Now, it was my older sister and me for my major learning years. See, a man knows all he needs to know to survive by age two. Oh, I have not mentioned this yet, but I was born in Mississippi. That is right, men mature faster if they are southern bred and born. See, the combination of the breeding and borning get you a better DNA quality that allows for maturing exponentially by two. This allows for a more efficient time frame from womb to work. Do not bother looking it up, it is just a well-known fact.

One of the things I learned early on in life is sometimes you gotta duck! OK, so the story goes something like this: "Hey, Mark, remember when you got your first set of stitches." "Well, by golly I do! I was in the process of chasing my older sister around the old truck in the yard." My sister was so much faster than I was at the time. See, at around three years old a man's legs are really just stumps with clogs attached. Therefore, we tend to pound around when we run. Which is good because it helps us get a good, steady bobble to our head as we move.

My sister, being a girl and a year (and a day) older, had her a real nice gait. I mean really, the girl can run. She had me by two laps on the ole truck. But I am not a man who sees defeat so easily. So, I thought to myself: *Self, if you just could shorten this lap by just a bit, we might catch 'er.* What my mind did not process during this evolution is that my mom and dad were on the tailgate watching this disaster about to unfold and poking fun at their losing son.

So, with the encouragement of their rousing, I kicked it on up into high gear rounding the front bumper with lightning speed. Tore past the driver's door stripping the paint off. I began to make the corner for the rear of the truck and instead of clearing the tailgate like I had done on previous attempts, I implemented my plan. It was all good in theory. Except the tailgate was right at eye level. Thankfully, though, my nose was there to prevent my eyes from being gouged out. Oh, what gusto I struck that tailgate with. My feet literally struck the tailgate as my head was stopped urgently.

Remember, I am man. I was made to take this kind of abuse. My body hit the ground, but my mind was still in pursuit of a win. I rolled out from under that tailgate. Stood up and wiped my face, slinging blood onto my mom, and took off again. I made my way around the truck only to be snatched up by my dad and dragged inside. This was not an uncommon thing for me at this point in my life. My dad had snatched me up several times by now and usually would give me a what-for later on.

The next thing I remember was the bath water running and my thinking was, *how did I get so dirty so fast.* But to my surprise, I was dunked under that stream of warm water and the sound I will never forget as long as I live – "Elaine! Get the damn car ready." (Another sound I became too familiar with.)

Just so you know. One thing that will send a man into panic quicker than anything is to see their father in a STATE OF PANIC. As my dad slapped a towel on my face and carried me out the door, I have to admit I got a bit teary eyed. The only thing I remember about the drive to the hospital was my dad using a few expletives followed by "idiot." At this time, I felt sorry for my sister. She was probably still hanging by the truck waiting for me to come back and eventually beat her. But remember she is smart, so I am sure she sat down and waited.

Now upon arrival at the hospital I remember the bed, I remember the doctor, and I remember there were some mumbled words. But what really got me was when he said stitches on my nose. I started belting out tears and cries like a wounded hyena. I had no idea what a "stitches" was, but geesh they did not sound good. There were people running in all directions solely off the fear instilled from those cries. Thankfully, my dad smacked some sense into me with a good, well, smack and a "Men don't cry" remark. I am glad he reminded me because truthfully, I had momentarily forgotten.

I really felt like I was on the verge of losing my nose. The skilled doctors and nurses were able to save it, although I do believe they had to use some special parts because my eyes had turned this god-awful rainbow of colors for at least the first thirty years of my life. The swelling was just crazy. I have only seen my face swell to that level a few more times in my life due to allergies and one beating I took.

So, when people ask me, "Mark, do you remember your first set of stitches," I smile and say, "Why yes, yes I do, you see this here scar across my nose, the way my left side of nose is different from my right, and how I have a rainbow of discoloration – let me tell that story."

One would think that I would be a bit wary of situations that involve the nose and stitches, or as referred to by us experienced folk, sutures, but I wasn't. It was not too long after that near loss of my face that I was introduced to the next lesson in life: Things are put in place to screw you over. Yep – this is the definition of pure tragedy and some with a weakness of the ole stomach hold back button have lost more calories from this event than a month on Atkins.

So, when people ask me, "Mark, do you remember when you tore your nose off your face?" I look them dead in their eyes and say, "Sit down!" I let out a sigh and pace a bit, rub my hands together, and begin. It was a hot summer day in Southern California. It was an odd day as the sun rose in the west and set in the east, as I recall. The clouds floated effortlessly as the smog blew past. In the distance, I saw a swing set calling ever so faintly: *Mark, come play.* And I ran towards the swing set.

Now as every red-blooded, yellow-belly, blue-bearded kid knows, swing sets are the definition of fun and excitement. Shoot, I was the king of sky flying. Stop it! You do not know what sky flying is? Well, my friend, that is when you get the swing going so high you can scoop balls of flaming sunshine up and throw them in your heart. You know when the swing has that moment of pause, and your belly jumps up and tries to take hold of your vocal cords. That right there is sky flying. I mean you have to master the swing to accomplish this, and it takes years for most folks, but remember I was born and bred in Southern Mississippi! This little niche will come in handy in the future when I tackle the launch. That is an altogether different story.

As any kid knows, anywhere in the ole world, swings are not meant for just swinging on. That is the beauty of a swing. There is the see-saw. There is a sit and talk place. Later in life there is a make-out place, come to find out (I seen people do it once). But the best thing a swing set is for is climbing on. That is right, a true jungle gym. You can climb all over them rascals from top to bottom. A talented scout such as I was well versed in the flipping and dangling opportunities that set brought.

It was on one of the events where tragedy struck. I climbed to the top of the swing. I flipped a few times. I hung upside down for well over sixty years, I am sure. Well, during all these fine acrobatics, my mom came out and yelled out those words every youngster loves to hear: "GET IN HERE AND EAT SOMETHING!" I am not sure if you folks fully understand how powerful Momma's cooking is to a growing man such as I was. My mom made THE best bologna sandwiches. I mean they were made to order just for me, mustard and all.

I got distracted, something one cannot afford to do when performing such aerial daredevil stunts such as I. But I did. A sandwich of some sorts was embedded in my brain as I attempted my dismount from atop the swing. I mean clouds were below me, I was so high up there. I was going to do the backward roll over the top dismount that I was so famous for, and fans demanded. I set myself up perfectly. Belly button even with the bar. Legs swinging heavily to and fro. And then … slippage occurred. The right hand/arm gave out first as my legs swung forward. A head tilted and then it caught me, ugggghhh!

Oh, wait, I need to explain to you the perils and dangers of being 65 million feet in the air on a swing set. No, no, no, it is not height! Why does everyone say that? DO you not remember I am from Southern Mississippi, born and bred! No, the danger is the stupid bolts that stick up through the piping to hold the cockamamie chains for the swings. Whoever was the design engineer on that certainly was not involved in quality swing set antics as a kid. That is right, folks. As my body slowly proceeded towards the ground with unrelenting speed, my left nostril seemed to find its way onto the screw protruding upward from that bar. You know most folks would call it a bolt, but I am telling the story, so it is a screw.

This is an extraordinarily huge screw. Oh my gosh, I felt it rip through my innocent flesh. I knew it was bad. I just lost my nose and my god, I just realized at that moment I only had one. NO replacement, no alternative! How would I breathe the rest of my life? All the hours of entertainment I had from picking that side of my nose alone were flashing through my tiny little brain. And then thump, a bounce and thud. I had landed on terra firma.

It is unmanly to admit, but I shed a tear at this time. Rolled over. Pulled my shirt up to my nose and ran towards my mommy. What happened? Nothing! My mom yelled,

"Let me see." At this point I want you to remember my mom was a nurse. She had seen some stuff. She worked in the emergency room. My scrapes and wounds, to this point, really had no effect. When I busted my nose on the tailgate – no biggie. When my mom saw this gaping wound – it was tragic. She let out a squeal of some sorts that I think was supposed to be my sister's name because she instinctively showed up.

I do not remember how my mom got me into her Mercury, but I vaguely remember the squealing tires, the passing lights and her yelling, "Hang on, son, you don't need a nose anyway." Well, that is my memory anyway. The same doctor that only months before had reconstructed my face was there in the ER and just passed out (once again my story, when you get your nose torn off you tell it how you like).

Luckily, I survived the two or three sutures I received. The bonus on this is that my eyes did not change from the current state of multi-coloredness they had been from the previous injury. Yep, life is like that for a man living in Southern California but with the genes of a pure-bred Mississippian. I learned a lot from that incident. Life is going to screw you if you get to playing around in the clouds too long and stealing sunshine balls. I found it is best to watch out for them things sticking out that just may screw you.

You know, my mom was a particularly OK mom. I mean I really did not need virtually any mothering once I exited the womb. I got a full-time job, provided for myself shortly after conception, and pretty much stayed that way my entire life. Sure, I needed the occasional routine transport to the ole medical facility for some mending. But that is only due to my short legs I had when I was younger. Other than that – SELF SUFFICIENT!

Except there was this time I got myself in a predicament that only a mother could help me with. "Mark, do you remember when I had to get you down from a tree?" "Yes, Mom, I do, ugggghhh." This is a very difficult story for my pride to tell. I mean at this point in my life I had fought Indians, for goodness' sakes! I served next to General MacArthur and drove tanks! I owned a fleet of dump trucks and earthmovers. I am a man's man.

There was this gargantuan spruce in our back yard. I mean this was no ordinary tree, this tree was 2 million feet tall and had branches the size of homes. I sat there one fine day and sized up the behemoth. I looked it up and down. I went side to side. I did some finite math inside my head. After studying the equations and taking into account windage and altitude, I knew this was no hill for a climber. So, I kissed mother earth goodbye and grabbed what climbing gear every man needs: sheer will and determination.

Now one judgment your mind might begin to form is that ole Marky boy is afraid of heights. I want to stop you right there. I can assure you that on this occasion, fear had no role in this mishap. This was the gods that be had a bit of anger issues and decided to lash out at the only man who could handle their wrath. ME!

I began my ascent, which was nice and easy. The branches were low and evenly spaced. I remember chuckling at the ease of my progress. This big ole tree was a teddy bear. An

ole softy. Sort of snuggly in a prickly sort of way. Oh, I had
the occasional run-in with sap puddles and ornery needles
jabbing me in the earlobe, but I trudged on through. I could
get a view every now and again through the thick foliage
the tree provided. On the way up I said hello to the owl, the
squirrel, and the singing robin. I passed through the first
layers of clouds and decided to don my breathing apparatus
(AKA kerchief).

As I made my way the view began to open, and I could
see beyond my neighborhood. I got so high up I could see
the Hollywood sign. Everything in nature was telling me
I had gone far enough, yet I defied with laughter any rec-
ommendation they had. I surpassed the sun, I am sure of
it. It became suddenly dark, and I could feel the sway of
the massive tree as it attempted to shake me loose from its
straining branches. We were entrenched in the epic battle
that all Southern Mississippi men know of – Man versus
Nature. I was not going to lose this battle.

I stepped up to the next branch and I will have you
know that this very tree spoke to me with a groan. "No
more," cracked out from that branch. But I am fearless, so
I proceeded. The next branch rang out the same warning –
"No more!" However, I did not slow down. "I am going to
crest your summit, you ole spruce," I snarled out. The next
words from that tree I am certain were, "Oh yeah!" I fell
past those last dozen branches. Luckily the ole spruce, now
referred to as Mr. Spruce, was kind enough to catch me in
some lower limbs.

Well, Mr. Spruce was a tad angry and was not letting

me move. In fact, he was shaking some sort of awful. I knew he was angry and I did not want to upset him any further, so I did what any red-blooded, yellow-belly blue beard would, and yelled at the top of my lungs, "MOMMY!" And right here I have to tell you, I have no idea where on the planet my mom was at. I mean, could have been in Antarctica for all I knew. Moms have a sense of hearing that would make a bat jealous. It is amazing.

My mom popped up at the base of this tree. "Mark, what are you doing up there? Come down right now!" "I can't, Mom, Mr. Spruce has me and he won't let go." "I am not playing, you get down here right now!" "Mom, we can do this all day, Mr. Spruce will not let me go. Can I use dad's chain saw for a minute?"

OK, that part about the chain saw was not said in the conversation, but my pride made me throw it in there. I heard my mom uttering out prayers to Mother Mary and Jesus as she approached the base of the tree. Yes, my mom is a devout Catholic. How did you know?

She began her ascent. Now this tree, Mr. Spruce, had taken me a better part of the afternoon to climb. My mom scaled this thing in seconds. Grabbed me by my collar and jerked me out of that tree and placed me on the ground. Yes, my mom was tall, five foot two. I was barely three feet something.

You know, come to think about, I really did all that for my mom. I cannot remember one bridge game or social gathering where that rescue was not a big hit for my mom to tell her friends. I gotta say I was a dern good son to take on that challenge and include my mom. She would not be the same today if not for me.

OK, OK, I know you want some Southern Mississippi stories. You have to understand that yes, I was born and bred in Southern Mississippi. But my learning years I spent in Southern California. I gotta tell you about some of the learning that took place, then we will get to the oasis of storytelling, Southern Mississippi.

Speaking of learning, hey Mark, do you remember anything from, let's say, kindergarten? Oh, I have two beauts here. One involves my mom again, bless her heart. Both involve some sort of poo story. Being that I was a man and all, I made my mom aware that there would be none of this dropping me off at school garbage. *Nope, won't have any of that. I am walking!* So, I walked. During school, I had met a like-minded, albeit Southern Cali, fellow and we decided we could walk some together. I was glad his house was first because I am a loner type of guy but wanted to make him feel special, you know. His name was Scotty.

Scotty and I would chat about junk on the way and usually discuss how to get away with biting the other kids. I really do not know what that was all about. I even had a report card that stated that Mark is doing well in school but still bites other kids. So, I was a biter, and I would discuss my technique with Scotty on the way home. Oftentimes we would have some sort of snack left over from our lunches.

Well, on this walk home, Scotty and I were trying to finish off some delicious cookies his mom made and chasing it with some thermosed beverages. We got to laughing and joking about the day of biting events when a whole heap of tragedy fell upon us. That is correct, how did you know? We dumped the cookies on the ground and with one fatal misplaced step, rendered it into a mound of crumbs. So, where does the poop come into play? We added the thermosed beverage to attempt to wash it off the side, and it looked just like dog poop.

Now you can say so or whatever at this point if you want to. But to real men, a pile a dog diarrhea in the middle of the sidewalk, well that is all out fall on your face laughter right there. Guess what, we decided to step really hard on the poop just to see what would happen. Well, we found out. Somehow, this vengeful, spiteful, nasty, malicious pile of fake poo decided to leap out from under our foot and end up on both our clean school clothes. How many moms out there just cringed up a tad? I bet one or two of y'all even whimpered a bit.

See, to a man coming home from kindergarten – he knew he could not under any circumstances dirty his clean clothes. In fact, it was fully expected that the pants be worn for at least three whole days. The laughter faded. Scotty frowned. The skies greyed. We began a frantic wipe to no avail. "What will we do, Scotty?" "I dunno, Mark. People will think we were pooed on, I know." Scotty said it first, the words that no man wants to hear, "My mom won't love me anymore." I followed with ,"Mine won't either."

How can a happy moment of eating cookies and a fictitious poo pile turn to such overwhelming morbid sadness? It was not a pleasant day to walk home alone, but

I am a man. I straightened my pooed-up shirt, dusted off my pooed-up jeans, and began my solitary march home. I passed a few neighbors who gave me that look. A few of the older kids just stared in astonishment as I walked the next 743 miles home.

Once I arrived, I threw my lunch box on the table and waited for the worst. I may have snibbled and sniffed a bit, but no tears. Mom comes in and what the heck does she say, "Get out of those dirty clothes, boy, don't be messing up my chairs!" Now, was this a trick? How could she not notice the poo-tinged clothes, the anguish and disgust I was wearing? I mean people surely had talked by now. What was this time warp I had slipped off into? Nothing more was said. Sometimes moms pick their battles.

The next day Scotty and I remained silent for the walk to kindergarten. We bit a few less people during the following week. We owed it to our moms not to create as much trouble as we were known for. I am thankful my mom still loved me after this incident. I am sure there were plenty of dirty clothes. My mom just had to say, "I am not even going to ask."

This next one is a bit short and not quite as funny, but it just goes to show how pretty OK moms are.

Like I said, I walked to and from school. I had no problem except one day. I had a really bad tummy ache. I think I may have bitten someone who was contaminated with the plague or something similar. This is not the day of cell phones and call mommy when you feel bad at school. Our school nurse believed that beating was the best cure for any ailment. No joke. I cut myself stealing some chalk from my teacher's desk. When I went to the nurse, she smacked me and told to me to pinch the crud out of my little booger pickers until the blood stops coming. She was really effective. I mean I hardly know of any kid that was sick in that class.

Anyway, I had to make that 2,398-mile trek across the most dangerous terrain man has ever thought of dreaming to think of in a thought. Oh, my stomach was killing me. I can remember at mile 4 million, things went from drastic to dire. I could see the entry to our neighborhood and that is when it hit me – poo pressure. Now I am older and have experienced this far too often. I have it on good information that it is a proven fact that your body will do anything to embarrass you at, or as close to, your home as it can (especially on a date).

Let me draw you a mental picture of what I see. A brick, flowered entry to my neighborhood. One on each side, and some small structure in the middle. Oh, the beautiful array of color. You can imagine the sweet scent of their nectar filling the entrance to the quiet neighborhood. On my end there was sweat flowing down my forehead. I was a small man praying like a Pentecostal speaking in tongues on a Wednesday night evangelical service. I quickened my pace with no intention of making it home, no not at all. I was a dreamer, but I was also a realist, and I knew all hope was slipping out of sight with each small step.

For some unknown reason, I stopped at the wall. Not only did I stop, I sat down on the wall. When I sat down on

the wall, that was an unannounced cue for my body to re-
lease its contents undeterred. I couldn't fight it. There were
too many miles, my legs were too short, and there was just
too much, well, crap. There were cars passing and I was just
sitting there pooing myself like a pro. Waving to the passersby and hoping the flowers covered the scent of the situation accruing in my pants. When it was all done, I sat there
for a moment. Not really proud of myself but reassured that
when a difficult decision has to be made, I can make it.
Sure, I might get a little poo on myself but my goodness, I
can make a decision and stick with it. So yes, some would
say humiliating, but me, I am forever the optimist and I see
it for what it really is.

I managed to hobble my little-legged self home. Pants
full of nasty ole poo. Mom opens the door, helps me to the
bathroom tub, sets out some fresh clothes, and sends me on
to my full-time job. What? I told you I am a pure bred and
born Southern Mississippi man – we start working before
kindergarten. My mom is amazing, no poo ever bothered
her. It was as if she fully expected me to show up with poo
in my pants.

CHAPTER 2

Reaching Home Sweet Home
Southern Mississippi

Hey, Mark, do you remember when you found out you were leaving that godforsaken Southern California? Why yes, yes I most certainly do. How can any self-righteous bred and born Southern Mississippi man ever forget that day?

Now, I was walking home one day from my full-time second job when I saw my dad leaving in his souped-up El Camino. Man, that thing was nice, 350/350 under the hood. It rumbled so loudly it shook my heart loose on two occasions. Oh, I almost forgot it killed a pigeon once too, or maybe it was just the fan. My dad was my hero back in the day. He stopped as I was waving him down, "Where ya going, Dad?" "Get home to your momma, boy!" "But I wanna come with you"? "You best listen to what I say." And he drove off.

I can see him downing a beer as he made the corner. I immediately interrogated my mom. "Sit down there, Mom! Where is Dad going?" "He is going to find us a new home."

MARK ALBERTS | 19

"Where?" "Mississippi by your grandma and grandpa."
"Yours?" She said yes. See, I told you my mom was pretty
OK. She was from Bay St. Louis, Mississippi. A Southern
Mississippi girl. Her dad was Sicilian and her mom was
German-Dutch (ugggghhh). But me, I am born and bred
through and through Southern Mississippian.

Oh, I counted the days for my dad's return. Which
he did. I knew you thought this was a pack of cigarette story, but not yet. We set the date, even decided to bring my
two sisters along against my wishes. We got a Ryder truck
and packed the furniture and loaded it up. My dad drove
that big ole truck like a dang pro. Whipping through the
towns and byways like he owned the place. I bet he drank
two or three cases a day and peed only twice. I really think
we lost Mom and my sisters somewhere along the Texas/
Arizona area. We arrived in Mississippi two days before
my mom and sisters. I shed a tear when I read off that old
Interstate 10 sign "Welcome to Mississippi – The Magnolia
State."

Home! I could feel it in my bones. Home, I tell you.
This was my DNA. You know I have been told you only
have one love in your life and this is it right here – humidity, pines, bayous, rivers, and the great Gulf Coast. Yes sir, as
a boy in the seventies, this is it. I was five or so at this time.
My dad and I made it to the rendezvous point of Grandma
and Grandpa M. This couple, I tell you. What a pair.

My Grandpa M was called Blackie because he was seriously dark skinned. He had silver hair and beady little
eyes with long eyebrows. Great guy, though not much of a

talker. They called my mom Janie. That was not her name. I guess that was their thing. To make up odd names that have no rhyme or reason to them. In fact, I do not even think I know that side of the family's true identity. I mean we had Aunt Mutt, Aunt Red, V, Bell, and so on. Hmm?

My mom and sisters arrived, and we made our way over to our new home. Gosh, when we saw that place it was awesome. I think it was like a billion acres (three actually). I saw horses and cowboys roaming around. My sisters wanted to choose rooms and I wanted the outdoors and come to find out that is where I would spend most of my days and nights. We got settled in and met the neighbors.

What I remember most vividly about that day is the tool set I received from Grandma and Grandpa M. Now, I had used tools in the past, don't get me wrong. I was using a hacksaw at seven months to cut conduit for my dad's electrical business. Some say I was a natural at it, but that was mostly those Cali folks. To be honest, I had a lazy pull back and you know that is where most of the cut comes from. Grandma and Grandpa M had gotten me a real life honest to goodness tool set.

I know most men are thinking it's good tools such as them stores that sell automobile stuff have. No sir, this was the finest the TG&Y had. It was a genuine blue-coated, wooden handle, made in somewhere outside the US garden tool set. That is right, it was the set, folks. I mean a rake, shovel, and hoe. Gosh dern, I was so happy. I held the tool set in my hands for a few minutes while I soaked up the goodness that the lord above had just provided.

Alright, so your imagination is going wild at this time, I am most certain. I know mine was. What do I do first? Hoe? Rake? No, hoe! Oh wait, shovel. So many options. No more of this digging in the ground with a stob or Mom's old spoon. (OK, I did use her good spoons that Thanksgiving Day.) *I've got what I am going to do. That is right! I am going to dig a tunnel.* I tossed the hoe and rake out of sight and found me the perfect tunneling ground.

I was a highly talented theoretical tunnel digger. See many nights I had fantasized about tunneling through enemy lines. I knew all about perfect shovel scoop size as to not wear myself out before peak tunnel depth. I knew the mound distance for the dirt has to be approximately 62.8-inch feet from the tunnel side or we'd risk cave in. I did not have any measuring device, but a shoe would suffice. Preferably, I would use the right shoe. My left toenail was about to fall off during this expedition and there was no way I was going to risk losing it.

I traced out my tunnel outline. Exactly 2,769 steps and three quarters long. The tunnel was going to be, oh I would say, about yay wide. Which, for you folks who don't know, is also known as just about right. I broke ground. Just dug right in there. There was not any ribbon cutting ceremony or the like. I dug and dug and shoveled and shoveled. I tore through roots and I tore through decaying animal flesh. I am certain I was in an Indian mastodon ancient burial ground. After a brief sign of the cross I continued the digging and the shoveling.

I think I was down near Beijing when I decided to cut

her hard right. Finally, the tunnel was being formed. I could see it. The traveling to and from buying my mom trinkets from Italy (since it was just to the right of China). Telling my sisters that they could not come into my tunnel and visit my friends in Mexico. (There are multiple branches now in my tunnel.) Oh, how I would be the envy of my new classmates. I dug faster and harder now.

During all this digging I felt a little rumble in my already frail rugged little man body. At this time, I did what every red-blooded, dirty-bellied, blue beard digging man would and called out for Mom. Oh man, she did wonders. Her classic but delicious bologna and mayo sammy. Gosh, the bologna even tasted better in Mississippi. I chased that down with a canteen shot full of cherry Kool-Aid®. Then back at it!

So, a bit more digging and I got tired. I realized that the hole was deep enough for me to lie in, and cool too. The tunnel was deep enough for me to fit my head and shoulders in. I made the decision: NAP TIME. Now, would you not know that somewhere during that nap time some sort of corporate espionage had occurred? I was lying there peaceful as a rugged man of my stature could get. When the earth above me began to crumble tad pieces onto my face.

The engineer in me ran some figures and briefly, I felt reassured. It was within a nanosecond of that reassurance that I realized the figures were not for this here tunnel that was collapsing around me. It all happened so fast, I remember. The small clumps fell first and slow. Then the large clumps. Then all at once the entire world fell in. I swear to you that I also believe the moon itself was sucked into that tunnel head and rested its weight upon my rugged little body.

My first instinct was to scream, and I went with it. That was a bad instinct because of all the great things in Mississippi, the dirt ain't one of 'em. I then kicked my feet as hard as I could. My thinking was the gyration of the fast twitch muscles would improve the situation. Although this was the first time I was wrong about this move, it would not be the last (sorry, Amber). It was at this very moment that I remembered something very critical: I need to breathe to live.

I swear by the ever-loving Indians floating next to me in that Chinese-bound tunnel, that I died at least eight times right there. If it were not for me being a born and bred Southern Mississippi man, I may have given up the ghost. But I looked death straight in the eye and I said … Who am I kidding? I was crying mud tears and asking Jesus if I could be his friend in heaven if I could get in. I started a Hail Mary but all I could get out was hhhhhhhhha…

My legs were twitching. Arms a-flailing. I think I peed myself. Then I felt something grab my leg with a god-awful force. The Grim Reaper, Father Time himself had latched on to me. *This was a good run*, I thought. One quick jerk, maybe two dozen smacks, punches and kicks, and there was my dad. I had never been so happy to receive a beating (at this point in my life) than that day. He cursed me for sure. Beat me more? Definitely. Then he hurt me with a gut-wrenching command: "Bury that god-forsaken hole in my yard, NOW!" I smiled, which got me one more back hand, but hey, I looked death square in the eye and through my muddy little teared-up eyes I said, "Ha! Fooled ya!"

You see, that taught me some things, that ole tunnel-building exercise. Remember cribbing if you are going to China via a homemade-dug tunnel. As a side note, a plastic bag over your face when you sleep may keep the mud out your eyes when you start to cry from being buried alive. Most importantly, though, those who save you may not look, sound, or even feel like a savior, but my gosh, they are just the same. Bless my dad's Old Milwaukee heart, he may claim he wanted to kill me, but when he had the chance, he passed it by. Maybe he knew I would do the job myself one day.

Being my dad was not an easy task, not at all. I feel the need to describe my dear ole pops to you. He was maybe twenty-two feet tall, big ole arms and legs, and the ground shook whenever he would walk around. He would clench your fist so tight during a handshake, your pinky toe would go numb. When he stood over me, the sun would be blocked out. Sure, there were bigger fellers out there, to be sure. My pops, though, he was the toughest.

My dad believed firmly that to raise a young'n boy up such as myself, well, beatings had to take place. I remember him saying during multiple beatings that he did this because "I love you." Other times, I knew he was in great pain because he stated several times that the beating session that was about to occur, would hurt him way more than it would hurt me. I felt bad for the old-timer. He must have been in pain a lot and must have really loved me to endure all those beatings I had to take.

Now, my dad was an avid fisherman. I tried my best to learn from him. There were several things I learned from fishing with my dad. One of the most valued lessons a kid can learn is how to properly retrieve and open a can of beer from the cooler. It sounds like a simple enough task, but skill and timing are required for the event to go well. You must understand that the boat rocks. Spilled beer was an unacceptable incident where there was no reprieve. Spilled beer definitely led to a beating of varying magnitude.

The beer could not be opened too early either. This would lead to premature flattening of said beer. A boy would have to count the steps to the deliveree of said beer. The beer would have to be snapped open at the correct sweeping motion of delivery. There can be no hesitation in the opening. The beer must be ready for consumption upon entering the hand of the consumer and not a moment sooner.

I made the mistake one time of misjudging the delivering. This is the day I found I can swim well over five hundred miles back to shore. It was not a normal day. The fishing was poor. The seas were rough as can be. Everyone was on edge, and I must admit I was one of the edgiest. I heard the call – "One cold beer, boy!" I flung into action. Countering the waves. Leaping over rolling debris. Navigating the deck through waters washing away the traction of my stubby little feet. I reached into the cold ice chest and pulled a can of the wobbly pop out and instantaneously headed the product to the intended dispenser. Upon arrival, tragedy struck.

I reached out the beer with my left hand. Right hand in the prepared position of tab pullage. The boat took a 150-foot rogue wave off the port-starboard listing side. My dear pops was reaching for his much-needed beverage when our hands collided. I saw it all in slow motion as the tab slid to a half open position. The brightly colored aluminum can began its terminal flight to the deck of the boat. One grab – one miss. Another grab – the can tumbles across my hand. I hear the cries of my dad and all the members on the vessel – ALCOHOL ABUSE! I landed hard on the cold, wet deck.

Disappointment overtook me. I saw what I assumed was a demon possess my pops as the can emptied its life contents on the very same deck. I felt the wrath of a beer-deprived demon take hold of the nape of my neck. I had no shirt on in hopes of a Coppertone tan developing. Now my hopes were set on survival. This demon convinced my dad to hurl me straight into the straits of the Gulf of Mexico. I did not know how to swim or speak Spanish. Lesser little fellers may have panicked in this situation. No, not me. I got all my panicking out the way while I was mid-air.

I am a quicker learner than most folks, being southern born and bred, you know. I seen this swimming thing done on many occasions. My technique I chose was somewhere between a dolphin, a dog, and a drowning cow. My first instinct was to make back to the boat. My dad persuaded me otherwise. So, I kicked up the arm flailing into high gear, set the left toe in rudder mode, and off I went to seeking a distant shore not yet in sight. Somewhere near nightfall I made my way onto the beaches of ole Mississippi. I knew my one love would not let me down. She gracefully guided me to her sandy bosom and allowed me a moment's rest before I set off to my full-time job.

Gosh, I really do appreciate my dear ole dad. You see he always had a way of showing me I could do things I thought were impossible. I never knew I could swim prior to that event. I mean not many four- or five-year-olds can survive a few feet swimming in the water. I made it well over 3 million miles though and still put in a full day's work. I tell you: my dad was awesome.

I loved his garage, as did my friend. I did say his garage. We were not directly allowed to enter that area without written consent from a current sitting republican president. On occasion though, the garage door would be up and my friends and I would be forever thankful. My dad had superb taste in art. He had Miss December 1974, which was our favorite, displayed in her unframed glory. She was a beautiful brunette with dark eyes right there on the wall. Then there was the blue-eyed, dark-haired beauty from August of 1968. There was the Lucy and Charlie Brown poster that taught us boys don't have to protect girls by swimming so close to them. Something about them sinking if Charlie took it out. I don't know what it meant, but we laughed at it.

Now, my dad got girlie magazines delivered to him once a month. Since it was my job to intercept the mail and place it on the table in the house, I would occasionally (monthly) review said magazines. Sometimes (always) I would share said contents of said magazines with my friends. This was not an easy feat. The timing had to be just right. One cannot just simply remove the magazine from the daily mail pile and then reinsert. No! I had two sisters who were eager to discover some misgivings on my behalf just to see how I would survive another near-death experience. I swear those two were betting on how many times I would shake hands with death and survive. Little did they know, me and death were becoming best buddies.

The proper etiquette for removal and particularly reinsertion of the nudie magazines is as follows. Upon retrieval of magazine from mailbox, look over both shoulders and all around for the presence of spies. Never attempt to detach a nudie magazine on a Saturday delivery. Don't ask me how I know, just for the love of songbirds, take my word for it. Once you have a clear and confident feeling of no spy-dom, slip said magazine up into your shirt. Find one piece of flyer mail you plan to leave on the table for evidence of mail service of that given day. Next – deliver contents of magazine and remaining mail to private members-only fort.

The fort must be well fortified with known members. Those known members will be contacted by special code or simply "the nudie magazine has arrived." Access must be granted upon verification of membership. The access goes something like this: "Hey Pete, look at what page twelve has." That was verification enough. We had highly advanced facial recognition programs in our fort.

The key is during the viewing process no one can damage the magazine or its protective covering in anyway. I found out how important this is on a very hot and humid day. We were thumbing our way through the July 1980 edition of the nudie magazine. It was extremely hot and we failed to recognize that the publishers must have changed the ink process. We were leaving fingerprints on the cover and in specific locations of the photos during our viewing. All my friends had left the fort and I was prepping the return of the magazine in the mail delivery the next day. That is when I noticed it. The plethora of lil nubby fingerprints all over the cover. I looked anxiously once more again through the smeared pages of beauty. The intellectual articles were each smeared beyond comprehension. How does one feller pull off the magazine heist of the century with his fingerprints blatantly screaming out his name. *Oh man, I may not survive this at all!*

I wrapped the plastic cover in pristine condition on the damaged magazine. I drank a huge swig of my cherry Kool-Aid from my canteen. I tucked in the safe spot for the night and made my way up to the house from the fort. All night I stared at that ceiling. All night I contemplated various countries I could escape to. Who had extradition laws, I wondered. The next day the sun came up (dagnabbit). I did my chores and around noon I made my way to the fort.

The magazine was still in its damaged state of fingerprinted disarray. I hoisted it up feeling the weight of sin I placed upon myself by stealing all the previous copies for my own lustful indulgence. As I placed it in the mailbox, I whimpered (not cried) a bit. The hard part began – the waiting. I sat there thinking of things to occupy my last day on earth but could find no solace. I was prepared to admit full guilt upon the questioning that was going to take place. I stacked bandages and made a walking stick. I told my friends it would be a few weeks of intensive recovery ahead and there was no use to wait around. I doubted I would ever be the same.

I heard my dad's truck making its way down the streets to our home. Ole Fort Bayou Road, then up onto Nix Road, making the last turn onto Kruger Place. The old trucked hurried home as to help tell the tale of my dirty deeds. My dad leaps out of the truck obviously perturbed by all the dumb folks he works with. Slings the door open with enough force it graciously closes itself behind him. Even the door was smart enough not to cross my pops. He heads to the table. He grunts as he flips through the debris of miscellaneous bills and advertisers. He yells out my name, "BOY!" I say, "Yes," in the most manly feeble way possible. It was almost a squeak of culpability. I snail my way into the kitchen where he is. There in his right hand lies the defiled magazine with my DNA all abreast it. I say, "Yes, Pops." "Get me a beer and ice mug." "YES SIR, right away."

Nothing else was said – NOTHING. It seemed we grew a little closer through that event. I never ever saw another one of his magazines first though. I had to wait until they ended up in a dresser drawer or his storage place for bygone nudie mags. From that day on he would say things like, "Keep your nasty meat beaters off my tools" or, "I ain't touching those bologna nubs." None of which I understood at the time. See, my dad is great. I learned a lot from him growing up.

One thing I learned the best way I know how, the hard way, was the relationship between a man and his car. My dad had a '71 Gran Torino with a 351 Cleveland. It was bored and stroked. Open headers and a shift kit. My gawd, boys, this had a four-barrel carb on it. My dad loved this car. It was his last connection to days of youthful bliss. He would work on this creature with the precision of a surgeon. He would caress each bolt, belt, and curve with the care and delicacy of handling newborn babes. The only time I ever heard "I love you" was when the car ran a 10.09 quarter.

My dad kept the keys of that vehicle stationed in the safest place known to him – the GARAGE! I in my infinite wisdom at eleven or twelve decided it would be awesome to surprise my dear ole pops with a nice clean vehicle. So, I did what any red-bellied, heavy-footed, soon-to-be-missing blue-blood Southern boy would do. I washed it right where it sat in the driveway. It was like the hose was made to reach the car and all. Soap to clean it was right there in laundry room. Access was easy. It would take all of thirty minutes to complete this task. WRONG! WRONG! WRONG!

I got to thinking how I drove the tractor on the farm. I thought how I drove the truck on the backroads. I thought of the numerous times I drove atop my dad's lap down public roads. I also thought of the times I rode in the front seat of that Torino with my dad. Oh, when that car started, my chest would thump right along with the lope of the cam.

That way I could not lean forward when he stepped ever so slightly on the brakes. The devil on my shoulder was whispering all the pornography of excursions I could have just moving the beast into the yard and back again. The unfortunate side of it was the angel was in full agreement.

I snuck quietly into the garage even though my dad was at work. I crawled onto that sturdy workbench that smelled of grease and marvel oil. You could almost eat that bench, it smelled so good. I reached out and grabbed the coveted keys. No one else had held that duo of Ford keys up to that point. Oh, that was victory in and of itself. On my way down I blew Ms. 1968 a kiss and glanced at Marilyn. I never had landed so softly on the ground.

I was giddy with excitement as I made my way out to the awesome specimen of raw horsepower. The door opened all by itself, simply inviting me in and saying hello. I must admit I felt no wrongdoing. The seats had soaked up the warmth of the Mississippi sun and then permeated my body once I sat down. It was a warm welcoming and further set my mind at ease. Everything was simply encouraging… No! More than that, this was meant to be a once in a man's lifetime event. I knew it!

I slowly inserted the keys into the slot. It was a respectful event. I did not want to waste it. I wanted to feel every centimeter (a word I just learned at the time) of its shaft slide into the keyway. Once the key bottomed out to its depth, I groaned and my heart raced. The moment we had all waited for (well, I waited for) was finally within reach. I turned the ignition switch and the beast sprang to life with a growl that belched out "Why has thoust disturbed my slumber?" I grasped the keys so as to let the beast know that I was now the commander of its destiny.

I pumped the gas pedal several high revs just to feel the vibrating horses under my seat. One hand on the steering wheel, the other at rest on the console shifter. We were prepped for take-off. All systems go. I eased the beast into reverse and smashed the gas. This is when I realized I had a big problem. I could not see over the seat. Yep, my altitude impeded my ability to determine at what point brakes need be applied. I said to myself: "Self, you are southern born and southern bred, you know physics and algebra. Shoot, there is no problem.

I began my formulation through the use of the quadratic equation and the Pythagorean theorem. I determined acceleration needed to reach the end of a fifty-foot driveway in ten-second car. The answer came to me, but not through resolving the equation. No, not at all. You see, there was a ditch across the street from the end of my driveway. Luckily, there was a mud-laden hill to stop the vehicle before hurling it through the wildlife refuge. I realized that I was not a math savant at that time. In fact, I realized at that very moment that I would not be much more than I would become by the time my dad comes home at 5 p.m.

I am not proud of what I did next. Not the slightest bit. I shut the car off and left the keys dangling in the ignition. Mud, grass, and debris were all over the back and sides of the car. The beast no longer growled. In fact it looked so meek and powerless set amongst the tadpoles and crawfish.

The smell of the mud cooking off the heated exhaust was the last thing I would ever smell. I took it in like the perfume worn by Anne Marie (a girl I crushed on in fourth grade). I couldn't do anything about the stains on the seat or the bend in the steering wheel. I knew this was my last day on this earth.

I went into the house and cleaned my shorts and butt. I read a verse from the Bible and began to figure out how to escape my fate. It came to me all of a sudden like. SERE training, I had practiced. For all you non-southern folks, that is short for I am so scared I am going to die I need to kick into high gear and practice survival, evasion, resistance, and escape. I knew I would need all my years of knowledge to live through this ordeal.

I felt too guilty to take any clothes my parents bought me, so I kept what was on my back. I loaded my canteen up with cherry drink, no sugar. Mom needed that for coffee. Some fishing line and my Rambo knife completed my ensemble. You are correct. I ran away as fast as my nubby lil legs would carry me. There was not any time for tears. NO! I had to survive. I started off at the bayou, where I took my fishing line and made some Indian hooks. Indian hooks are small pieces of tree branch where you sharpen the ends and tie the line in the middle. One then would shove the hook inside of a grub or worm. The fish would eat worm and all. I would eat fish and all.

Off I set on my adventure and my new life. I began thinking of names. I believed I would call myself Steve. I enjoyed Steve Austin and felt I had some bionics in me.

Steve it was. I arrived at the bayou and set my line and began a fort construction. I was a tired feller at this time, so I laid to rest for a bit just off in the woods. When I was awoken by this terribly familiar sound. A rumble off in the distance that could only mean one thing. They found me! How? I covered my tracks. I took alternate routes. I left all identity behind. These folks in this neck of the woods only knew me as Steve.

The rumble and grrrr of the ole GMC approached where I was. Out stepped my pops. I believe he was carrying a high-powered rifle, a fully automatic military rifle, and a bat. He knew I would not go easily. I checked my inventory and realized all I had was a Rambo knife. "Ughh! MARK!!!!" Rang out throughout the bayou land. The wildlife became silent as we all shared the fear that was beset upon the region. "BOY!!!" Was the utterance of how sincere the situation. I popped out the woods. "Yes, sir?" I summoned through the tightly clinched vocal cords.

My dad asked me straight forward: "Did you wreck my car?" I replied as affirmatively as I could muster. "Y-y-y-es, that was me." I told myself, *No tears NO TEARS. Get in the truck!* I did as I was instructed. My dad clinched the steering wheel as he sat upright in the cab. He took a swig of beer. I fidgeted with my fingers and searched for words. My dad looked over at me and said words I will never forget. "Son, I am disappointed in you, not because you wrecked the car but because you ran away. Southern born and bred men do not run away. We stand and face the consequences."

I was punished for sure. Nothing I could not recover

from. Although my dad's words rang true, I am ashamed to say there were a few more times I ran away from things. I eventually got to where I stood my ground despite the consequences. Sometimes the hurt was significant, but nothing was ever as powerful as his words. Oh, I did help get the car out of the ditch. I did not catch any fish on the Indian hooks that day. My pops sold that car eventually but managed to let me stay around. It all worked out in the end

CHAPTER 3

First Friends and First Loves

I have to tell you all one thing about me that has stayed quite consistent throughout my life; the woods are my first love and my best friend. I can get lost in the woods and never panic. Well, except that one time. I swear Sasquatch and three youngins were chasing me after skinny dipping in the Okatoma River one fall. Back to where I started, though: I love the woods.

Now, I had friends just like everyone else, I assume. Next door to me were Tina and Raymond. Then across the street were Jamie and John. Then there was my bestest good buddy Pete and his family, God love 'em. Wendy was somewhere close to Pete, and then there were some other kiddos in the neighborhood. SO, when the neighborhood kids and I first met it was a love/hate relationship. I firmly believe to this day that those kids loved to hate me. They did not trust me because I still had the stupid Cali stench on me. They saw right through to what they conceived as my façade of Mississippian heritage.

I was going to have to prove to this clan of heathens that I was pure as the inbred Dilahunts. I was Mississippian gosh blessed and I was gonna prove it to them once and for all. I went to Jamie first. He kindly imparted a black eye and bloody lip. Next, I went to John, more blood from the lip and a huge Easter egg on my head from a wrap with a pine limb. Next came Pete. At this time we were still feeling each other out, so yes, he beat my tail too. I obviously was not any Mike Tyson. I dern sure was not any Usain Bolt either. I was a dern good George Foreman. I knew how to take a beating while landing some good licks in.

Yep, while there was a beating occurring, I would wait until the right time to let out an ear-piercing, bone-chilling, blood-curling cry that would call to all moms in the neighborhood. OH, you mock me now, but remember I cheated death already. How was I to know how many times that could occur? Therefore, I cried a bit from time to time for survival. Except the time Tina smacked me for trying to hold her hand. I cried because she broke my heart (insert and sigh here).

To give you a bit of perspective on what I was facing on just the individual level of each of these predators, I will give you their official beat down stats. Jamie was in fourth grade to start off. He smoked cigarettes and drove a real car. I once saw him change a tire out by lifting the car with his left arm and breaking the bolts and replacing the tire with his right arm and teeth. He slayed this giant in school one day with a simple combo to the gut. Which, thinking back, it took more than that to get me to cave.

John, he was lean and tall. He was deceptive. One moment you could be chatting about hot wheels and wham, he'd throw a jab out of nowhere and usually some blood would pour from a newly developed gash. At the bare minimum there would be significant bruising. John had one sore spot though and that was his dad. He never wore underwear and always wore shorts. His balls would occasionally peek out the cut-off short leg and just embarrass poor John. I would always pray his dad would step out during the beatings.

Now, Pete, although he became my bestest good buddy, he was tricky. See, he would sometimes wait until you were pinned on the ground and then wrap you with an upper cut or some deadly blow. Every now and then, he would just hit you because you were within arm's reach. I tell you one other thing that would just make your blood boil, all the girls liked Pete and never noticed I was there in the room.

As you can see, each one of these guys was a formidable force on their own. I faced them as a killer gang. I am sure at this point you are taking back all the nasty things you were calling me for crying. I was a born and bred Southern Mississippi man, by golly, and I had to prove to them just how crazy I was or else these beatings were my future. One day it happened. The gang rode up on their fully-raked Schwinns and banana-seat BMXs and plotted my demise. As they ran up on me in a fit of all rage, I could feel the bruising and breaking starting just from sheer expectation. But then crazy broke loose!

I grabbed the shovel I had (thanks, Grandma & Grandpa M) and began twirling it around like a mace. When I noticed that was only going to hold them off for a short period due to my weakening arms, I threw the weapon in the complete opposite direction. They watched it fly way out of sight and they giggled, or maybe it was a sneer. Things had gotten foggy after that. No, they did not get me, because I did what any red-blooded, yellow-belly, bloody-bearded scared-to-death child would do – I screamed as loud as I could.

This time I began to run as fast as I could. I had gotten three good steps when I looked back, and no one was chasing me. Now it must have been the relief that blinded me, because the stars as my witness, I did not see the side of the house fast approaching. I collided with that brick wall with all the force a fifty-pound object traveling at four million miles an hour could muster. When I came to, Peter, Paul, and Jamie were standing over me and my scraped-up face. I think they were honestly amazed that I had lived through the event.

It was really part of my plan all along. Once they were convinced that a solid brick wall could not create any lasting damage to me, they just plain lost all hope. My sisters came running outside mad as all heck because apparently, I knocked their pictures off the wall. My dad was mad because he swore I damaged the foundation. Me, I slept so well that night and way on into the next day. Besides suffering from the occasional headache, I am …what was I saying?

I bet you are wondering where Tina and Raymond come into the picture. These were our next-door neighbors. The neighborhood I grew up in was divided into three-acre tracts. The houses were spaced roughly 250 to 300 feet apart. Most lots were slightly wooded, but there were woods all around us. Raymond was Tina's younger brother and Tina was close to mine and Pete's age. Tina was a gorgeous Panamanian girl. Dark skin, dark eyes, and dark hair made her so perfect. We would all play bikes and dirt track along with some other games.

Mississippi has its fair share of rain. It also had these craters in the ground that would fill with that there rain. The ditches would become rivers that any brave soul could attempt to jump with their bike or leap across. Those water-filled arenas would end up being some of the best playgrounds we had growing up. Not to mention the wildlife they had attracted, from snakes to crayfish we enjoyed them all.

My first skinny dipping affair involved Tina and one of them craters that filled with rainwater. It was all very innocent. It was the average hot, humid day in Mississippi. Tina and I had been playing explorer out in the north forty. We tromped through some ditches and crossed many ravines with deadly wild varmints. It came to the part of the day where we had one of them deep craters to conquer.

We splashed around in the knee-deep puddle. Tina suggested it was time to do the laundry and she needed my shirt. I was about seven or so at this time. To me, there was not any sexual ideation floating in my head. In fact, Tina was the only girl who did not have cooties in my mind. She was just like one of the crew. Without hesitation, I took my shirt and handed it to her. She swished it around in the dirty water.

Next, she asked me for my shorts, so I handed her those too. Next, I know, I was taking a bath in the dirty ole water. Though nothing could be seen, it felt funny and exciting being naked there next to Tina. I was not smart enough to ask Tina to do the same. Like I said, I was not thinking along the same level as I would today. The event had taken all of thirty seconds. Another common theme I seem to have inadvertently adopted when dealing with women.

I loved playing in the water. I am Pisces through and through. I have pulled frogs and snakes from the murky deaths, and a few crayfish and several thousand pollywogs. One expedition turned terribly sour real quick. I was attacked horribly and viciously by a turtle one day. That is correct, a turtle attacked me. I swear it was rabbinuos.

I was in the process of exploring the back forty where there are several million deep holes where all sorts of critters exist. I was deep diving one of the holes with my snorkel and swim fins and came across this ancient turtle. This species was particularly interesting and the scientists in the neighborhood (Pete, Tina, Raymond, and my sisters) would be keen on examining it.

Before I continue this story, it is very important to understand that when a turtle clamps down on any limb, they hold on until it thunders, or they die. This is a well-known scientific fact that has been studied in-depth in the local Mississippi science department (mentioned above). Also, every turtle has enough clamping force to sever a frog's head and remove human legs without any strain. These are deadly, conniving animals.

This particular turtle was no exception. We went face to face at a depth of 1,000 million feet. I snagged him up and we engaged in a brief battle of strength and will. His little legs just a-kicking. He snapped his jaws wildly. It took all I had to hold on to the thrashing animal. This beast was extremely feisty, all four inches of him. Do not let the size deceive you. I have personally witnessed how four inches can cause serious damage or intense pleasure. Size is just part of the camouflage this beast used.

In the midst of the snapping jaws, I was distracted by the need to breathe. I broke the surface of the water and that is when I felt the pain of my mistake. Clamped down on my left thumb was this four-inch, two-hundred-pound rabies-infested beast of a turtle. I was at the back of the property, nearly four hundred miles of sprint ahead of me. I took off trying to refrain from panicking. I could feel the beast gnawing through my thumb and rabies injecting into my arterial flow.

The first person to see me with this beast on my thumb was Raymond and he began to cry. He apparently saw the strain I was under as my right arm was shaking fiercely from holding the beast and my left arm. Or maybe he recognized the infamous sweat and blank stare from the rabies pulsing through my contaminated brain. Tina saw the atrocity and screamed for her mother. At this time, I was beginning to hallucinate as I swear, I saw my mother running at me with a ball-peen hammer.

The hallucinations must have spread to the beast as it released its death bite as it appeared my mother was getting closer. I do not remember much after that as the turtle venom had taken its toll. I believe I had passed out at mile marker 249 and eventually came to on the back porch. My thumb was gone, amputated by the sheer force of the beast's jaws. I could not see it from the large amount of bandages on my left thumb stump.

My mom, Tina, Raymond, and my sisters were there staring at my deformities. I could not even cry because Tina was there, and I did not want her to realize I was no man under this rugged exterior. Make no mistake about it, I was crying on the inside. My thumb was important to me. I wanted to hitchhike to cowboy land one day, for goodness' sake.

I stuttered out the question to my mom, "How much is lef le left?" She replied, "What?" The turtle, he is fine, he retreated once he let go. Poor little fellow." I was like, "No, my thumb, is it there?" Everyone laughed! "Yes, you just got a nasty cut. I think God made it thunder and that is why the beast let go.", Tina is positive it was my mom crazily waving the hammer. My sisters think it was that my thumb tasted nasty, and the turtle spit it out. Raymond just kept quiet. Later it was told he has a fear of turtle stew.

I know the truth really. It was a bit of divine intervention. God had made the perfect born and bred Mississippi man and that strikes fear in all living beings. See that turtle tasted the blood filled with my DNA and just could not handle the level of perfection.

CHAPTER 4

It's Elementary!

Now that I had left ole Cali, I graduated to a real school system. No more Kindergarten for me; no sir! I was now part of the academia known as elementary school. You know what the best part of joining the school system is? No, no! Not the socialization times. It is the new sneaks you get. You see, buying sneaks is a very important time for a man. There is a testing process. See, sneaks are designed categorically for specific young fellers.

Now, picking out a set of sneaks required precision and a predetermined checklist. The wrong set of sneaks could lead you into a danger land that is too frightening to discuss. The first test sneaks must go through is the flexibility test. You have to grasp the sneak on each end and then flex it like you're Stretch Armstrong. A little feller really has got to put some effort in on this flexing. You skimp on this, and you won't be able to hurdle any cliffs or mountains, that's for certain.

The next test is where a lot of the learning from kindergarten comes in. The ole grip test is perfected during the former years. The test consists of several layers. The first being the heat-up phase. The wearer of said sneaks in question must attempt to run in place, on linoleum floor preferably. The run must not be a casual run, NO! You must put some serious effort spinning out in place. Good sneaks must squeak or squeal but not, and I repeat must not, create slippage that would lead you to fall down. If that happens leave the store immediately, well, after you take the shoes off.

Once the sneaks are properly attuned, stretch out a bit and pick a good run lane. The purpose of this test is to ensure the ability to change direction at high speed. See, fellers tend to get themselves into predicaments that necessitate high speed maneuverability. Poor sneaks could lead to pummeling that need not happen if the right zig to zag ratio can be maintained. The test is simple enough, Mom or Meemaw (an aunt will do in a crunch, thanks, Aunt Mitzie) will count down the launch. The tester (me) will run as fast as possible with a stop and turn. If confidence is built during this phase, there is an attempt to stop abruptly and run in the opposite direction.

See, I want you to notice that I purposely listed specific duties to Mom, Meemaw, or a trusty aunt. There is a reason a feller does not want his pops around. See, pops do not need to see how you perform in the gear meant to run from his beatings. No! Sneaks have got to be like a secret weapon. Never under any circumstance do you break out all your sneaks' capabilities during a beating either. No matter from pops or from other foe. Just use one, maybe two special functions at the most.

Another reason why you need the listed authorized test partners on site is in the event of test failure. I had more than my fair share of department store tragedies. I was at the TG&Y with Mom and Grams one fine day getting sized and fitted for summer sneaks. During the testing phase a pair of sneaks failed miserably, leading to wreckage and carnage only a mom can handle. A dad would have lost it. I mean I skinned both knees and my chin and took out two shopping carts. It was tragedy all around. I am not sure, but I believe it was in the papers and evening news.

Now you may have noticed that I did not mention the look of the sneak. To a feller, we don't care about no stinking looks or style. We know we are going to get poked fun at no matter the style. We need to think about the getaway and stay puttin' the sneaks bring to the table. That is it! The best pair of sneaks can act like Jesus in a serious all-out fire fight. You literally can walk on water with the right persuasion. You do not believe me? You just have not been in the right circumstances.

I can tell you about a time me and my ole pal Pete made the fatal mistake of being without any sneaks, much less the right sneaks. See, we were out late one night sneaking around ole Amy's house trying to get her attention. It was dark and of course after an episode of M.A.S.H. We tapped on her window, or so we thought. Well, Mr. Amy's dad came out of the house with what we swore was a bazooka and hand grenades.

Now, behind Amy's dad's house was the Amazon Jungle. We headed in there to evade the madness and wrath that was sure to be upon us. We had made no such plans for evasion. This was a simple recon mission. Nothing more. Shoes were not supposed to be required. We were too deep in the jungle to turn back when we both realized we had no sneaks. Pete did not care because he pushed down over the briars and ran across my back. Luckily though he reached back and drug me across the briars and into the road.

Well, you know Mississippi is a relatively humid state. On this particular night it was a balmy 92 percent humidity and as I began to sweat, I felt every bit of the briar patch's retribution for me breaking its slumber. Pete had no visible wounds. I learned two valuable lessons that evening. First, always wear your sneaks. They are there to save your life. Second, knock on the front door, not the back window. It takes the edge off everyone.

Now another important part of getting ready for school is the lunch pail. I mean really, do you want to have the old traditional pail with some silly cartoon? What about the practical paper bag? Do you want to drink school milk or will you canteen your beverage of choice? Very important choices to make and they have to be made wisely. Remember, I still had to prove I was southern born and southern Bred.

You guessed it! I am brown bagging it all the way. I loved the brown bag lunch. When the room was minimal in my cubby (or pocket), I could mash the contents down to fit just about anywhere. The drink was a very hard choice though. I love milk and I love chocolate milk but unbeknownst to me, I was lactose intolerant. Oh man did that leave me in a bind on more than one occasion. We will get back to that in a moment.

I think I may have mentioned it, but my mom knew how to make a sammy especially for me. I mean her peanut butter and jelly were divine. My favorite was braunschweiger and grape jelly on white bread. Let's not leave out her bologna and mustard sandwiches too. See, my mom was the best. No doubt. All these sandwiches could be manipulated into just about any shape and still retain their ever-lovin' goodness. Nope, no chips. Chips were for those fancy kids and my sisters, as were the cookies.

Now, more than anything, brown bag lunches are part of a smart feller's strategic and tactical planning. No one, I mean no one, wants to steal a brown bag lunch. One time ole Tommy D. stole my lunch. Now, I just laughed to myself of course and I did not use any of my sneaks' capabilities. Why, you ask? Because that was braunschweiger and grape jelly day and no soft kid like ole Tommy could handle a man's meal like that. Tommy met me about halfway through lunch and threw the sandwich and a left hook into my gut. Afterwards, I just ate my braunschweiger and grape jelly sandwich and enjoyed every bite.

Now you may have noticed there was no long spill on picking out the right garb to wear. Rough Country or Sears brand stiff blue jeans and some sort of shirt would suffice for me. Haircuts were crew cuts for me (thank you, Dad). I mean who is going to school to make a statement. The learning had to be done so as I could get better at digging tunnels and jumping my bike across the Nile or Mississippi River.

There was this one time though I made the ever-loving mistake of wearing a *Star Trek* T-shirt to school. Oh, I am not sure if I mentioned I may have added a tad bit of lie about the shirt. Yep, I said I was on the cast of *Star Trek*. Who would be the wiser that I wasn't right? Geesh, Ms. B, my teacher at the time, really tried to set the record straight. She asked me, "Mark, are you sure you are on *Star Trek*?" That's right, I said.

"Who's the Captain?

"Kirk," I said.

"No, who is the actor that plays Captain Kirk?"

"His name is James T. Kirk, don't you know?

"Oh, brother!"

"No, that is Charlie Brown, ha, ha!"

Well, she encouraged the kiddos in the class to pester me with all these questions I had no answers to. Which led to me telling everyone I lied about being on *Star Trek*. Which led to me being beat up on the playground by several people, including a few girls. A terrible day for me, for sure.

But I did get Ms. B back. One day we had to clean out our desks. I polished mine up super special. In fact, I wanted my desk so clean I stuck my head on the cubby to blow out the far corners. I want everyone to know at this point that all kids have huge ears compared to their heads when they are younger. It is a medical known fact that you are born with the same size ears you have as an adult, and you must grow into them somewhere in your nineties. Having said that, my head became stuck in the desk cubby due to my ears hanging up on the edges. Please remember I did have that tragic tunnel incident happen to me just a short time ago.

Now, at first, I did not panic. No, that panic did not set in until I would say the first five or maybe ten seconds. At first, I assessed the darkness of the desk cubby and how close the walls were to my face. Then I realized that I could not turn my head side to side. Then I realized that I was on my bad side and could not remember which side that was. Next, I did what every red-blooded, flat-belly, blue-bearded kid would do in this situation. I succumbed to the darkness. I did, I admit it. It was life or death I tell you I had to make the call. HELLLLLLPPPPPP!!!!!!

Oh, Ms. B came running over there and that was a feat for her. She was not very light. I felt her grip the desk with both her mighty hands. "Lawdy Jesus, Mark! What are you doing?" "Well, Ms. B!??" (At this point in time I actually doing a lot of praying. See, my mom raised a proper Catholic boy, at least when the times a called for it.) "Get your daggum head out of the desk right now," she yelled. That right there gained the attention of the entire class. I remember Debbie hollering, "Yank him out by the feet!" Christian was crying in the corner in terror. Several students sounded like they were trying to exit the room.

Ms. B said, "Y'all stand back now." She grabbed me by my waist band and jerked so hard my ear just about separated from my head. I was out but being beat on by Ms. B. Apparently there was an arterial bleed from where my chin struck the floor. I could not speak for a moment but just as I was about to thank this angel for saving my life, I noticed she was Satan incarnate. Her eyes were glowing with embers. "OUT IN THE HALL," she exclaimed. What?? I could not believe this, licks for getting my head stuck in the desk and a mucked-up chin to boot. Who would have thunk it.

I remember my first-grade teacher, Ms. Cummings. She was awesome. I really think she liked me because she held back when giving me licks. Wait – you don't know what licks are? They are paddlings, whoopings, beatings. I know they are not allowed in schools today, but they were all the rage in late seventies and all through the eighties.

The funny thing about licks is that as a red-blooded, yellow-belly, blue-bearded kid you deserved to be beat at least four times a day. The reasons need not be discussed. Just trust me, I would be worse off had I not received the due punishment. I want you, no, really, I need you to understand. As hard as it may be to comprehend, I was not the perfect kid you see painted in the paragraphs of this here book. Hard to believe, but let that sink in.

Remember Jamie, my neighbor, well he still went to the elementary school I attended. He was in fourth grade, and I was in first grade. Just for fun he decided to celebrate my 100th formal beat down during recess. In return, I earned a series of licks for obliging Jamie with a body to beat on, which led to the authorization of licks. Thankfully, Ms. Cummings was the one rendering the licks. See, Ms. Cummings did not have the paddle with the holes. Ms. B. and the principal both had paddles with holes in them.

What is so special about the aerodynamics of the holed paddles? Well, the physics allows that resistance is reduced to allow for acceleration to be increased. I know force equals mass times acceleration. I learned that while running into walls. Well, even though a holed-out paddle lacked mass, it had plenty of acceleration! One cool thing about holed-out paddles though is they break far more often than solid paddles. I know I have had both broken across my bunkus.

There was an incident during nap time where I found a pack of Certs and began eating them. Well, I found them at recess on the playground and really have no idea what they were. When I was questioned about the whereabouts of their origin, I politely submitted the truth. Ms. Cummings was upset to say the least. She told me I could die eating things I *just found*. To prove her point, she issued a long series of licks. Needless to say, I survived paddlings and exploratory eating events.

The irony of getting licks at school is that the news travels fast to your parents. Once you got home, that is when tragedy occurred. My dad firmly believed he was robbed of his duty to beat me first by some sniveling teacher. That thievery had to receive recompense in form of … you guessed it – more beatings. My dad was not as withholding as Ms. Cummings. My dad would hold one of my arms and beat me in circles. There was no sense crying because a southern bred and born man just does not cry. Oh, and Dad would prove that by beating until the tears stopped.

Now parents, they don't necessarily have the paddles lying around the house. I have been beat with everything from pillows, towels, and belts to the occasional wrench. The worst thing that happened with the beating episodes was not actually the beating. Those were done in a relatively quick fashion. The worst part was the wait. Parents would play all coy and deceptive. At dinnertime the beatings would not be announced. It was like your last meal was being prepared.

Everyone at the dinner table spoke casually. All the politeness and pleasantries of the day. Then as the dishes were being cleared and bellies were all full, the judge laid out the sentence. "MARK! You received licks today in school, didn't you?" "Yes, sir," would screech past my paralyzed vocal cords. "Go get my belt, broom handle, baseball bat (or whatever device the beating was going to be dealt with) and wait for me in your room." More waiting. Staring at the device that was going to expel a 250-pound man's wrath upon parts of my body I am certain were not made to take this abuse.

"Now son, this is going to hurt me more than it hurts you. I have to do this because I love you. When that speech is given, fellas and fellets, do not respond with "Yeah, yeah, let's get it over." I beg you, for the love of green grass and BMX bikes, don't say any version of that phrase. In fact it is best just to whimper out a single snivel of "I'm sorry."

The night I made the fatal mistake of saying that phrase in an audible fashion was a night I know my father meant to cause bodily harm. It really was not my fault. I usually kept those type of comments sequestered in the depths of thoughts.

The moment those words slipped past my lips and landed upon the ear socket of my dear ole Pops, my life was forever changed. The man lost it. I mean I had watched every episode of *The Hulk* up to that point, and no such damage had been done to a single human as this man was doing to me. He flung me around by my heels, then my arms, occasionally landing some shots in here and there. I am sure he was speaking to me, but I could not make out what he was gnarling out.

Blood, spit, and brain matter spewed across my room. I finally had enough and in my head, I said, *Enough*, but I believe I was unconscious at that point. The paramedics said my mom broke up the carnage and I was a lucky little man. They applauded the fact that not a tear had fallen from me, but they had all been shook out. It took a full night's rest to get over that beating. Once I recovered though, my dad obliged me with the beating I missed for the beating I got at school. Thank goodness we got all caught up. I could not have endured waiting for the beating owed.

As you can see, school is tough for a feller. I liken it to becoming a SEAL in the Navy, only harder. I mean there is some sort of PE for at least six years. You constantly have to do things you've never done before, and they are hard.

The teachers want you to do good, but they sure have fun when you mess up. There is no quitting in school though. Believe me, I tried. It is where I learned that I don't have a choice and quitting is not an option. In school you learn how to deal with bad guys, the bullies. You have to learn to navigate the terrain, and many times in the dark. Heck, I grew up in Southern Mississippi, so you know we swam to school 95.876 percent of the time. Yep, if you can get through school you can get through SEAL training. It's a fact.

You want to talk about specialized warfare. Sit on the perimeter of any recess session on any day. The gals are out there planting seeds of dissension, which leads to the next uprising. The fellas are just waiting on the next attack mission to some poor ole passerby. Each attack is a risk. If not carefully planned out, you will succumb to the weaponry unleashed upon you. I had the luck of being on both sides of the field. I won some and lost some more.

One day it was noted by the gals that I had a crush on a certain female asset named Anne. Well, Anne did not share my adoration and was quick to let the squad know. The squad then in turn notified the highest-ranking battalion leader, Wayne. Unfortunately, Wayne liked Anne way more than I did, come to find out. Now, to tell you how sneaky them gals are, Anne would talk to me on the phone alluding to the likeability of Wayne. I would try to point out my finer points to her. She in turn would leak information to her squad. That leak would spill out to Wayne.

Wayne came directly at me during recess. I was at the disadvantage here because unbeknownst to me, Wayne had been gathering intel and forces to alleviate me from the playground. All playground fights start the same for most folks. Wayne came up accusing me of said infractions. There is the denial phase, then maybe a little pushing and tussling, and it ended with a few blows. That right there is not my style. I already said waiting for beatings is miserable.

Wayne approached me and began laying out his case for why he felt the need to take my life. The crowd added their what-for into the mix. I searched the mob and saw them gathering in. Mid-sentence I decided to throw a jab at Wayne and follow it by a left hook. That's right, I went straight to blows. No need for idle conversation. We can chat any time in the boys' room. I meant business. I threw a few more wild punches, jabs, and combos. Then out of the blue I felt it. A solid right balled-up fist straight to the old nose.

UGHHH! Why the nose? You can't do anything when hit in the nose. I mean that hurts like hades. I had to pause to evaluate the pain that was surging through my face, which gave Wayne the moment he needed. He leaped onto my back and drug me to the ground. He commenced to beating on my sides and head without any signs of mercy. All I could think about at this moment was my mom was going to kill me for dirtying up my school clothes. I managed to wriggle one hand free and sock Wayne in the ear. I did that several times in a row.

Now, the important thing to know about playground fights is that there is a time limit. Sooner or more like later, a teacher would have to break it up. Don't get me wrong, those teachers loved to see a good playground scrap. They would even bet. So, as I was beating Wayne with my left hand on his right side, he pummeled me with both hands. I honestly was just trying to make it to the bell.

See, the unwritten rule is you cannot cry in any fight. It just can't happen. You will never have any friends or family if you cry during a fight. Another rule during the fight is don't quit. You throw punches. You wriggle around. You dodge and evade. You do not QUIT. Now, I am not saying I have never run away from or during a fight. There were a few, but I found out from those experiences that it is better to just stand there and take a beating than to run away.

Finally, the teachers came over and broke us up. We both got detention and our parents were notified. The thing I loved most about any fight is that once it was over, win or lose, each person had a newfound respect for the other. You may not necessarily like each other, but there was respect. Wayne went on to date Anne and, well, I did not. I still crushed on her until … well, I guess I still have a little crush on her as I write this.

As a result of this, my dad went out and bought me a two-pair set of boxing gloves. We would tussle with those gloves on. I used to get so angry because he could whip me so easily. He would just knock me down with ease. One day in my rage, I yelled at him, asking why he never let me win.

He told me, "Son, you are better than that. You don't need anyone to let you win, one day you will be able to beat the tar out of me. Right now, you just have to earn it." I take that with me with all I do now.

CHAPTER 5

A Southern Boy Gets Around

There are few things as important to a growing boy as how he gets around. Growing up I did not come from a wealthy family. I know it is hard to believe when you consider my suave and debonair ways. It seems as though I come from an affluent life. I did not. That is not to say that my parents did not give us the best life they could. In fact, I would not have had it any other way. Everything I encountered has made me what I am today. Thanks, Mom and Dad, oh, and Aunt Mitzie, Uncle Dolphy, my Peepaw ... OK, well, you get the picture.

When I think back to the purchase of my real first bike, I distinctly remember it. I ain't talking no three-wheel, guided assist, plastic-wheel machine. No! I am speaking of a high-quality rugged two-wheel mobile machine. This machine would be capable of traversing the hills and prairies of Southern Mississippi like a Tiger Tank.

My pops took me to the Otasco. The Otasco store had

everything, so being able to visit the Otasco was more than I deserved on most occasions. They not only sold new bikes; they also had used bikes! I knew exactly what I wanted. Knobby tires, that is it. I did not care about anything else, just those rugged-looking treads. I had all kinds of plans I was going to accomplish with this newfound freedom. I ran to the first bike that met my criteria. No, son, that is not in your price range. A whimper slid over my vocal cords but dared not make an utterance. That would cancel the purchasing event.

I had no idea what that price range was. I was a six-year-old on a mission, so I shrugged it off and went to the next and got a great big NO! Dern. My dad had found this dilapidated, white used bike in the back for like $10. Now mind you, at six you can retire from the receipt from a $10 bill. I felt like I was purchasing a Corvette. I mean my goodness, Dad had found a bike and the tires were knobby, sort of. So I said sure. Gosh, he was the best.

My dad said I could have it as long as I could ride it out of the store. OK, here was the kink. I never been on a dang bike in my life at this point. I mean a trike, yes. But a two-wheel stand-alone bike, no siree. Now, I rolled the bike out of the rack and out into the aisle. I was surprised by the sway this machine had. I mean it literally swayed from the bent rims.

I stared at the beast of a bike. I envisioned the life it had with its previous owner. All the fields it had ravished, the wheelies it performed, and the girls that swooned. The seat was a mountain at about chest height. One full pedal and one bolt for the go-forward activators. The braking system was a mash handle without any cables. I threw my leg up and over the ball breaker bar, upon which sat my entire future reproductive system. Unfortunately, I was not very tall.

I could feel the anxiety of future failure rising up. I ignored it as I had learned to do in situations such as this. I threw my right foot onto that go-forward peg sitting at about the two o'clock position. I focused in on the width of the Otasco aisle ahead and the unwary shoppers. I took a deep breath and threw all 47.8 pounds (21.6817153 kilograms) of bodily thrust into that right leg and that mochine (pronounce moe sheen) leapt forward.

I was amazed at the velocity with which it thrust into action. The sway/wobble of the wheels became so obvious to the causation. I could hear my dad sounding off with salutations of what I was sure was pure pride on his part. His son riding his first bike straight into the Otasco display window. I am resilient though, and so was the bike. We practically broke nothing. I mean my dad did most of the damage slinging me around the store. I was amazed how me, and that bike, were one as he whipped us back and forth like a flag blowing in the Mississippi breeze. We were obviously meant to be.

Now, having a bike is a huge responsibility that most six-year-olds would not care to take on. There is the washing and the chain oiling. The hours you have to spend learning tricks and jumping rivers. I am not just the average six-year-old, however. I am after all a southern born and bred tougher than nails six-year-old. I don't mean to brag, but I became known far and wide for my bravery on that vee-cycle I had acquired due to the wealth of Father.

The first thing I learned how to do real well was, um, er, OK, I learned to fall very well. Do not underestimate the ability to fall well. It will serve you through your entire life. I got so good at it, people would try to imitate me and bust out in laughter when they could not fall as well as I. One such time I proved my efficiency at falling was in the midst of walking the wheelie mile. I believe I have spoken of the unique sway my mochine had. Well, this became a bit of a challenge when trying to stick the wheelie landing.

It was a late fall evening, and the streetlights were starting to flicker into life. The bugs were anticipating the light show and were awaiting about mouth level. I had popped a perfect 10.25 wheelie from the seated position and was walking her on down the matrimony aisle. I thought I would spend the rest of my life on this wheelie set. However, to keep from showing off I decided to set her on down at mile 247. In the process of leveling off, I came through a dense cloud of bug coverage. That prevented the proper air density to land the vessel per the user instructions.

Now, you may not fully appreciate the sway this bi-wheeled traveling machine had. I mean each revolution of the casing would change latitudinally and longitudinally the travel of the bike, and thusly the rider. The wobble from the sway, however, gave this particular vehicle a perpetual motion of sorts. That is, until any operator tried to manipulate the direction of travel. See, the slightest shift in the steering mechanism (i.e., handle bar) considers serious geo-metrical and calculus mathematical equations to be solved, ON THE FLY!

Now, being a highly qualified and experienced operator of this bi-wheel vee-hickle of course allowed me to be able to conduct the above mentioned mathematical calcs. What I failed to take into the equation this particular time was the density of said bug cloud and how there is some sort of alteration to the time space continuum. When the wheel touched down ever so slightly, my body propelled forward in such a manner that everyone witnessed time travel.

Not only did I recognize my poor little life flash before my eyes, but so did all the onlookers. Luckily, up to that point my life had been a series of comedic events and I al-lowed the spectators to laugh through this traumatic event. At the pivotal moment when I reached maximum velocity, I remembered to tuck and roll. As I remembered, my body was in a different position altogether. I was fully stretched out except my legs were somehow at ear level. The ground was approaching ever so quickly.

I felt it. I cannot lie at all. When I hit the earth and bounced, the earth tilted by 25.689 degrees on its axis. We had an actual eclipse that no one but me witnessed. I set several world and Guinness records that day. Unfortunately, there was no one there who could certify the event. I flew around the atmosphere three times prior to impacting the earth. I slid through asphalt, shell drives, and a ditch a total of 2,798.4 yards. After coming to a full and complete stop,

I walked away with minor bruising, scratches, staph infection, and a case of ringworm. Not sure if I already had the ringworm, though.

You all must be wondering how did the bike fare from all this skullduggery. We knocked the sway almost straight. The chain tightened up a bit and we tore a knob off the ole casing. It was a tough bike for sure. The people knew it was the star of the show. It could never have happened if it weren't for the fabulous bike and that incredible sway. I did get beat for the torn jeans and dirty shirt, but hey, that was just another day in my life.

You know I put that ole bike through the gates of hades and back. Thank goodness we both were and are Christians. I don't want to bore you with all the adventures of ramp jumping, trail blazing, barn jumping and unicycling it. Wait, are you sure you want to hear about the last two? I mean people have lost their lunches hearing about the unicycle event. Some have passed out cold and went on to meet their maker from the barn jumping event. OK, if you insist, I will tell you about those and then we'll lay this bike thing to rest.

So, directly after the great wheelie incident, repairs were in order. I broke out my dad's finest tools he had available. I flipped that bike over. Laid out said tools. Got the trusty oil can because this ole gal deserved some lube and my gawd, she was going to get lubed. Where to start adjusting and correcting was the question. Now mind you, I am working with the skill of a neurosurgeon. I have no instruction. Only sheer intuition and whit are on my side. It was up to me to make her better than before. Better than she thought she could be.

I mean I was building the million-dollar bike. Every kick of the pedal I would hear d-n-n- n-a-a-n-n-g-g just like Steve Austin. Pedals tight? Check! Chain oiled? Check! Front wheel? We can rebuild it. Two 9/16-inch nuts removed. Check! Wheel off and rolled around the yard successfully. Check! Place tire back on fork. Check! Oil back gear. Check! Flip bike over. Check!

I was on a roll. I mean for a feller who never did any kind of bike maintenance, I did great. I went the extra step and washed the ole girl up and patted her dry. I was so gentle not to knock any of the added features (AKA rust) off. I mean that is what made her unique. Well, that and so many other things.

So now comes the test ride. Man, I jump on her and we are off. I am pleasantly surprised how quickly she wants to full out run. I hold the reins a bit tight to keep her from opening up too soon. Hold! Hold! Hold! NOW! Down the hill and around the corner. Oh man, what a mechanic I am. I am so close to light speed. I feel the earth shake a tad when we breach supersonic. I love this bike!

Now comes the moment. The real test. Up to this point I have been gentle. But we need to see what this girl can really offer. Wheelie time. The true test of agility and endurance. I slow slightly. Lean forward a tad. Position the trust accelerator to the two o'clock position. Countdown 5-4-3-2 lift-off. I bet all of you at this moment see the issue. Who was supposed to check off the bolts being reinstalled. I wish

I had friends like all of you who yelled, "Don't forget your nuts." You would have saved me more times than you know. Truth is just one friend would have been OK at this point.

There I was front end in the air when I looked down with such a grin. Proud of my mechanician skills. Oh, how that changed so quickly. I saw the front tire continuing on a forward trajectory totally different from my own. Who could blame it. It knew exactly what Macbethian tragedy was about to be told. *So long, fair friend,* I thought. I am not easily overcome by fear. I have faced death more times than any six- or seven-year-old should. I have come out somewhat the victor each time. This time will be no different.

I performed some serious NASA calculations for proper launching and trust to weight ratios. All to prep for the upcoming gravitation swing that soon will be taking place. I could easily have walked this to the end of the earth, but the missing front tire shifted the air-foiling effects of the structure. This resulted in gravity being able to overcome the bike frame directly proportional to concern growing in my mind. Countdown 5-4-3 dagnabbit landing.

There was no tuck and roll for this landing. To say it plainly and simply, I wrecked in tragic proportions. I ate dirt, literally. I broke a thumb, literally. I had a cherry that extended the entire surface of my perianus. That is right, all around my butt was scraped raw. How that happened, I do not know. I swear I broke my cranium but my mom says it has always been that way. She should know, she was a nurse at one time.

Now it was my neighbor, Mrs. Huff, who saw the collision and heard my screams. Those screams were to inform others to clear the path. Nothing more. She ran over to me. Never had I been so happy to have a stranger of sorts pick gravel out of gaping wounds. Now my mom and dad were not so caring. Another pair of clothes ruined. Another trip to the doctor's office. Hey, but no cast or anything. Funny thing is that when you have a small fracture of the thumb metacarpal, they wait until the next stupid thing you do to see if you can break all the way.

Needless to say, it took me a couple of days to get the nuts back. The bike was a giver and just kept getting better with each dose of terror of I gave her. She did not know the word "quit" and only asked for more. It seems those gals are just not ever satisfied or can get enough of me riding them.

I mean take for instance the barn jump episode. I forgot which show I saw this occur on, where the feller took a perfectly good motorcycle and drove it out the hay door in the barn. You know, that kind of action TV goes straight to a little feller's head. That is why the eyes are so close to the brain. Stuff you see goes right in there. I saw the barn jump and determined, *I ain't scared. I am going to get this thing did.*

I went out to our barn and climbed to the hay loft. I think it was about 750,000 feet tall if I remember correctly. Just shy of needing any chute to decelerate my fall. I calculated that at a speed of a couple hundred miles an hour, give or take, I would land about right there and chucked out 3.25 bales of hay as a landing pad. I would use old baling string to hoist the ole gal up to the loft.

It took a minute to get the ole gal up there. She had put

on some weight as she was getting up in years. So, I took a little longer than usual. OK, I never hoisted her up there before and honestly, she still looked fine with the additional ten or so pounds. I drew out my plans there on the loft floor all in my head. I knew the runway distance, the required ducking needed to clear the hay chute opening, and the landing technique.

Luckily, my mom and dad were at work. I did not need their fear seeping into my certainty. All in all, it was the perfect summer day for this event. I would call it a stunt, but nothing this perfect could be considered such. The sun rose in the east and would set in the west. The view from the loft was such that one could see the clouds across the valleys below. The lark and mockingbird sang their songs of praise to the Lord above and all was right in the state of Southern Mississippi.

It felt right when I perched myself upon the seat of that ole gal. I placed that thrust adjustment tool upon the peg. I must admit the anticipation allowed for a slight rattle in the ole thrust adjustment tool. I checked all the protective gear. Yep, the bales of hay still lay below. Here we go, take off. As you know by now, this is where some reflective thoughts enter my brain. I realized there was no way I would get up to the speed I needed in that distance. Another thing I realized was there was not enough time to effectively terminate the jump and replan.

I was out of the hay loft opening looking straight at the ground when I realized I had only had elementary math and should never have relied on my calculations for placing the hay bales. I also realized that the absence of gravity, at times, could be a welcome effect. I also learned that contrary to science, terminal velocity can be reached relatively quickly. Additionally, terminal velocity is subjective based on the person or thing falling. To this day I have no idea how I passed up the bike on the way down. I did and I saw it happen. I mean I really saw myself in midair overtake the bike in a race to the ground.

Just so it is clear, I was not really trying to race to the ground. My full intention is that me and ole girl would be safely touched down to Terra Firme via the wheels so delicately reinstalled on her from above mentioned episode. Oh my goodnight underwear, did it hurt when I hit the ground and lawd, did it hurt when ole gal landed on top of me. It must have been the ten pounds I noticed. There was no air in the body I once had occupied. I was literally face down on the ground with nothing to break my fall except, well, me. I broke my fall.

The farm animals, including Budweiser, our Herford bull, were all pondering what just fell from the sky. I would like to come up with some clever way of how I shook the earth, but this was not at all the case here. I was hurting. I could not tell anyone 'cause, goodness, I just barely survived that incident, if indeed I did. If anyone would find out about this stunt (yes, it is a stunt now), I would surely be killed. I am not sure how long I laid there, but eventually I did get up. It was the end of ole gal. She had a broken frame weld right at the steering apparatus. I may have wept a moment for all she endured. I don't recall if any words were uttered or if I was even breathing at this point.

I feel I must take a moment to explain to all the fellets the various wound types us southern feller's encounter. I can only speak for southern fellers, but this may apply for some of the tough rascals up north too. This information is highly top secret and is not meant to arm you gals with any ego bullets to harm us ole boys. Use it wisely, ladies, please. The first type of wound is basically the shake it off wound. Now, the shake it off wound can vary in severity. I mean a feller could sever an appendage in the right crowded setting and that would be classified as a shake it off wound. There is some proven mathematical equation to the shake it off wound. You see, one simply takes the square root of the hypotenuse of the initial wound, applies the quadratic people around equation, and finally a coefficient of alcohol consumption, and there you have the shake it off wound.

Take this into consideration. Your man is working hard out in the yard all day. You notice at night during the romance of the evening, duct tape, old T-shirt material, and some silicone covering his lower calf. Upon questioning he responds to you, "Oh honey, the chainsaw sort of clipped my calf, but it stalled before sinking too far into the meat." See, he shook it off. No one to see the wound, work to be done, no alcohol, and plenty of ways to control the bleeding. Yes, the lesser person may have needed stitches and something to stop the arterial bleed, but southern men shake it off.

There are times when, ladies, an old feller just needs

some womanly attention. We do it to keep you gals interested and feeling useful. We southern men are a thoughtful group. Usually, the injuries you ladies will see are very minor with the ability to throw in a high degree of drama to it. These injuries are called the wine and cheese injuries. You probably seen an episode of this injury type and haven't paid it no attention. That is because you were lured into your caretaking nature.

A wine and cheese injury will look like this. A feller comes into the house and says nothing of the injury. Blood dripping or an appendage missing, maybe even a bone sticking out. The feller will make it obvious that he is hurt in some subtle way like bleeding on your favorite quilt. You may just find the clues of severed digits or an appendage laying on the dish-drying rack. You will come in and say, nice like, "Dear what is this blood doing on my favorite quilt." He will respond in some way such as, "Don't want to talk about it," or, "Ain't nothin'."

Next is where we hook you gals. We will moan and/or groan almost to make a whimpering sound. You may see the appearance of a tear just forming off the dominant eye. You are going to jump right and say, "Honey, you need a doctor, or some medical attention." We'll never go but we will complain about the wound and state it was the worst injury sustained to date. It would even be better if we were hurt doing something you asked us to do. You've heard it before. Honey, all I wanted to do is fix that broken disposal for you. I had it working and noticed the blade was loose while rotating. I could have finished it if I hadn't lost those two fingers in the tightening process. Yes, we would like some wine and cheese with injury!

Now, next is the I've been hurt injury. Ladies, I want you to know that a southern dude will lay down his life protecting you and any family around. I mean I seen a southern feller mowed down to the molecular lever with a machine gun. I have you know that each particle of that man kept fighting and overcame that unsuspecting enemy. His family lives to tell the story at every church event. So when you hear your southern man utter to you or any person or people, "I've been hurt," you get yourself in gear and start getting the specialist you need to put your man back together. I guarantee you he is already visiting the other side if he spoke those words. I pray I do not have to give examples of that one, because it ain't purdy.

Now, the last one is the top secretest of secrets. It is the oops I F'd up. See, usually this injury is done during the undertaking of something that should not be spoken of. This was the barn injury. I was hurt. I wanted my mommy and I wanted to cry. I could not though. Believe you me, had I pulled off the event, everyone would have known I done it. However, I did not and I needed to cover my tracks.

Now I was hurting, make no mistake about it. I had a welp on my right arm. I could not take a deep breath in. My mouth and nose were bleeding, and my entire body was stinging like fire ants had bitten me all over. I first went over and sat on the hay bale. I assessed the ole gal once more. I sort of laughed for a moment, probably just thankful to be alive. I stood up and grabbed the hay bale and when I jerked on that thing to slide it towards the ladder, I got a serious pain across my chest and into my shoulder blades. That sucked. I needed those bales back in the hay loft because I couldn't take a beating from Pops tonight.

It took me until late that afternoon to move those bales back in the loft. I still had chores of feeding the animals and taking out the trash. I was quite a bit more mobile though and found ways to move without hurting. Shallow breaths and not raising my arms above my shoulders was key. My mom got home and must have noticed I was sluggish. She asked if I was OK, and I said, "Yes, of course." I soaked in that tub for the longest time that night. I know my parents and sisters thought I was up to boyish shenanigans. But I just could not move too well.

The next day was worse because the bruising set in. Boy, was I bruised. I mean from head to toe I literally had some sort of bruise. My back was bruised and I landed on my front. I could not bend to tie my shoes, and putting on my shirt was misery. I sucked it up, ate my oatmeal and headed out the door for some more summer fun. Well, I went to my fort in the woods and rested some more. It took me a while to heal, but I got to say I was quite proud looking back. No one knew what had happened. Only me and Budweiser. Oh, and a few chickens.

Now the ole gal was in bad shape. My ole pops noticed her one day when I was trying to ride her around. She just did not heal as well as I did. My dad yelled out, "Hey youngin', get over here." I got nervous and began brainstorming ideas of how this may have occurred.

Bike finally gave up, did it? She was old anyhow, bound to happen," he stated. I was shocked. I thought to myself that this was the precipice to a volcano erupting. He never spoke anything about it. He helped me dismantle her and we put her in the trash.

After a year of riding my sister's ten speed, my father found the best getting around thing any boy could want. A Shetland Welsh palomino pony. What? No, I am not going to tell you about the time I hit a stop sign on sister's ten speed. We are going to talk about my pony. Her name is Dolly. I named her Dolly because I was going to marry Dolly Parton and Jaclyn Smith. I knew nothing about polygamy laws. Her full name was Dolly Jackie, but I called her Dolly.

I tell you Dolly was ancient. I mean she would tell me about watching the pyramids go up while pulling the pharaoh's chariot. I loved that animal though. She and I had some adventures. I had no saddle or bit bridle. I had a halter and baling twine to steer that mare across the wild plains of Southern Mississippi. That ole hussy would bite and buck just like me. I will admit, she could kick a feller way harder than I ever could.

The trio of me, Dolly, and Sam (my dog) was the terror of the bayou. Early in the mornings I would strap on my Rambo knife with my embedded fishing kit, a sammy of some sort, and a canteen of cherry Kool-Aid. I usually did not have sugar in the Kool-Aid, only the mix. I did not have any time for that foolish mixing and whatnot. Occasionally, I would catch my mom writing down a description of what

I was wearing for the day. I swear if she had a Polaroid, she would have snapped a shot. Later on in life my mom would confess to me that she wondered if I would come back from some of my excursions. Oh Mom, ye of little faith! I am a true blue born and bred southern boy.

On one excursion I had to teach Dolly how to cross a waterway. I was planning on navigating the bayous once we had this down. There was a small pond along the power lines across the street where the training was to begin. I had ole Dolly wound out as fast as she would go. That equates to about the speed of sound to the 9th power. She was fast for a trotter. We made our way along the power lines where all the mud booging trucks would attempt to run. Many ended up stuck, but not me and ole Dolly. We trudged on through the mush like tanks.

I gave Dolly a little tap on her brakes and jumped off her back as we approached the pond. Sam knew why we were there, and he jumped straight in and gave Dolly a how-to on navigating the waters. I grabbed on the bailing twine reigns and tugged that mare with all I had, but she refused vehemently. I jumped in to show it was all good. What a thought she must have had, an ole dog and a crazy man splashing around in an ole stagnant pond. She was not convinced this was a good thing.

I continued to try and persuade her by getting behind and trying to push the heifer. Dolly had about enough of that convincing when she belted me with a swift kick from her right hind leg. Lucky for me I was close enough that she managed to hurl me like 750 feet into the soft, muddy rut. *Stay calm, Mark, stay calm, Mark.* I went over to this devil-possessed creature and gave her a what for in common man language. I snatched onto that bridle and pulled with all my might. Dolly reared back her head and slung me upon her neck and then began to wail around. Now I am a true cowboy. I want bucking and broncing, but not while hanging up under this beast.

I was raised Catholic, so I knew the incantation for the exorcism rite of which I recited directly. She calmed down somewhere between "the power of Christ compels thee" and "Lord help me." She and I made another plan, which was to walk along the side of the pond and never mention water crossing again. In fact, we tried to avoid the power lines altogether just in case that demon was still lurking around in them woods that possessed her.

Looking back, I feel a bit sorry for ole Dolly. She was strapped with a young southern boy in his prime. Dolly was past all that nonsense for sure. There were days she'd handle the load (me) quite well. Others she certainly gave me what for. Dolly loved the sweets and treats I'd give her. I stole sweet feed that was meant for the cows and pigs just to ensure she had extras. I cut up my bologna sandwiches to share with her and Sam every outing we went on. Sugar cane and apples seemed her favorite, but they were limited.

I would watch my favorite TV show, *The Lone Ranger*, and head out to practice my hijinks with Dolly and Sam. I set up a five-gallon bucket to allow me to leap onto Dolly's back. I cannot tell you how many times I face-planted into some part or another of poor Dolly. She'd reward me with a swift kick to some random part of my body. On the rare occasions that I made it up on to her backside, she'd give a little buck or two. She only did that to see how committed I was. If I stayed on, we rode a bit. If I fell? You guessed it. A swift kick to a random part of my body.

We had a few cows on our three-acre farm. There was Anabelle, Budweiser, Steaks, and a calf named Michelob Lite. My dad was a beer drinker ... OK, my dad was a drinker. I guess he wanted people to know he was serious about it. Most of the animals were well aware of my capacity for roping, riding, and wrangling. I could catch piglets and chickens with ease. Rabbits were of little consequence for me. I outran most of them. Big Tom, our turkey, needn't worry with me. We had a special friendship and understanding.

One day after attending a rodeo in Bay St. Louis, I decided I needed to try my hand at lassoing and steer roping. I first discussed this with Dolly and she seemed indifferent about the ask, so I proceeded. Keep in mind I had no saddle, no real bridle, bailing twine as reins, and not a real lasso. I had a section of nylon rope that I am sure my dad was using to hold down something important. None of that stops a born and bred southern cowboy.

I hopped onto Dolly with rope in hand. A slipknot allowed for a nice circle for the unknowing candidate's head to slip right through. Michelob Lite was the target. Dolly had the perfect canter that would lob you unsuspectingly right to your prey. I placed the noose around Michelob's head and reared back, tightening the rope around that

300-pound calf's head. When I regained consciousness, I was being pulled at lightning speed through the pasture. I was so thankful that I had tied the other end of that rope to my right hand.

Now my mom was working in her strawberry patch. Usually there is no distracting her when she gets entrenched in her strawberries. It must have been the dust and manure that was flying in the field that first caught her attention. I heard her begin screaming, "Let go, Mark, just let go." I am no quitter though. My goodness, I was out to wrangle this here mongrel despite his fierce opposition to the idea.

I started pulling my way up the rope. I eventually got to the point where I was directly in the path where his back hooves wanted to travel. I thought I could trip the dern animal like I would do my sisters and unsuspecting friends. I simply would slap the back legs. Nope! Mission failure. Dagnabbit. No back-up plan. I could not get any closer due to the hooves beating my face in hurt. Well, as much as you could hurt a southern born and bred …

Suddenly Michelob stopped. That is right, he had succumbed to the superior power lurching on the end of that rope. No, no, not me. My pops somehow came from out of his garage den and snatched that calf by the rope and stopped him cold. "Get the hell up, son. Do you ever think?" I shrugged. I mean how do you answer the obvious. That was a well laid out plan. I was covered from head to toe in poop, grass, and cherries. Not the edible cherries. The cherries where half your hide is missing. I swear Dolly was sitting there smiling at me. She saw the potential.

Ole Dolly provided me with many trips to the bayou and adventures around the ponderosa. She ran away for a brief period of about six months. She returned older than she ever was and just not that into riding or frolicking. We eventually gave her to another family who had even more acreage and of course a set of youngsters ready to learn to ride. I swear Dolly looked at me with an *oh brother why me* look as she slowly entered the horse trailer. I can't lie, even though I am a true southern born and bred feller, I almost shed a tear.

Of course, as I got older, I had motorized vehicles and they each had their own adventures with me. Maybe I will share those in the future. We always remember our firsts though. I bear the scars brought on by both the old gal (bike) and Dolly. I am forever grateful for both of them. Although I am a little resentful, I never did get to ride ole Anne Marie on the handlebars or bareback with Dolly. Oh well, her loss for coming in the picture so late in life.

CHAPTER 6

Influencers

As I grew up from a little feller to a bigger feller, several people waxed and waned through my little life. I am not just talking about the Lone Ranger, Baretta, or the Duke. I mean real life people who helped steer me in, well, let's just say a direction. Not always the right direction, but a direction.

A feller would not be anything without their pops. Make no mistake. Whether good, bad, or everything in between, being a pops is a serious role. You know, my dad had a lot of faults. He was angry and drank too much. But he loved me and did the best he could. Most of my childhood I did not see that. Somehow though I always idolized the man, not the imperfections. I saw what he tried to be. As an adult I recognized his struggles and knew we all have them. I never was close to him. In fact, we never got to know each other at all. I do feel blessed to have him as a dad though. I really became the man I am today because of him.

In school I got picked on a bit. I think it is an initiation that little folk have to go through. The first time I was to get in a fight was around first grade. I was on the playground and just wanted to hang around Debbie and traverse the monkey bars. I think a senior in college came up to me and began shoving me and making fun of me. He smacked my face a bit with simple slaps. I quickly ran away and found a solid hiding place. I remained there, missing the bus home. I had the teacher notify my mom to come pick me up.

Over dinner my mom made me explain the situation to my dad. I missed the bus because I was hiding from another feller. My dad smacked his hand down on the table and looked dead at me. "You coward! You never run away, never." I shakedly explained the humongous size of the behemoth that was trying to beat my tail. I was suddenly taken up by my shirt collar. My mom yelled out, "Mike, you are ruining his school shirt." She was always worried about those type of things.

It was dark outside and slightly cold when my ole man tossed me across the damp grass. "Get up," he said. I did just that. "Come here." I followed that command as well. Smack, his open-palmed hand knocked the fat slap out my cheeks. Another one, and another one. He shoved me to the ground and demanded I get up again. I did and was quickly pushed back to the ground. Now, I was not hurt at all. I want you all to know that I had a bit of a temper back then, it just took a minute to let it loose.

After about the seventeenth time I fell to the ground, the switch clicked, and I came up without the command prompt. Both hands wailing sporadically. If I am honest, I was hitting myself more times than the air. My dad yelled, "Are you mad? Of course! Hit me." At this point I was both excited and afraid. I did as was instructed and struck my dad in the arm with a sloppy-fisted left. It sort of resembled a hook or maybe a half upper cut. My dad hit me with a hard closed fist punch to the sternum. Air escaped every orifice of my body.

As I was trying desperately to regain the breathing sequence I come to enjoy so much, my dad leaned in. He asked me very calmly, was that fellow as big as him? I squelched out a quick, "No sir." He said, "Well, if you can take this from me you can take it from him. Every time you run away, you will have me to deal with. You stand your ground."

Later my dad enrolled me in boxing at the YMCA. We practiced at Point Cadet Plaza. I sucked at boxing and excelled at getting beat up. I stayed in the training maybe six or eight months. Then I moved on to flag football. We did not have the money for both. Thinking back, I wish I would have stuck with boxing. There is a lot to learn from stepping into a ring where the outcome depends highly upon your heart and skill.

My mom on the other hand was averse to anything that could cause harm. In fact, everything could kill you and send you to hell in her eyes. You want to talk about opposites, her and my dad were it. She was a devout Catholic. My dad, agnostic at best. My dad loved nudie books. My mom swore that nakedness was of the devil. Everything we did was weighed on how fast it would get you to hell.

"Mom, I broke a chicken egg." "Oh my, you are going to hell for taking that unborn chicken's life." "Mom, didn't we have fried chicken last night." "Mark, you are going to hell for talking back to your mom."

I am a risk taker by nature. My poor mom had to endure a lot. She was a nurse for a period of time. God definitely knew what He was doing when He made her my mom. Not that my sisters (specifically my younger sister) didn't give her some grief. For instance, my younger sister decided to stick a pitchfork through her foot while cleaning up after a hurricane. I seemed to have a knack for creating excess worry in my mom's life though.

My mom never did succeed in creating a cautious bone in me. However, she gave me the passion to help others. One day we were heading down highway 90 heading to the country when a little girl got struck by a car in front of us. We witnessed the entire thing. My mom calmly asked my dad to pull over, which he did, and she walked out to help that hurt little girl. Did you hear me – she walked! I had witnessed this woman scream at me for my minor cuts and bruises but in this life-or-death situation, she walked over to help.

It was amazing. I could not see all that was being done. It all seemed so carefully orchestrated. The firemen doing their thing. The police directing traffic. My mom rendering aid to a stranger. They placed the little girl in the ambulance along with what I assumed to be her mom. My mom retrieved a shoe that was in the middle of the highway and handed it to one of the officers on scene.

She then walked back to the car and, once again, calmly sat down. "Thank you, Mike," she said. My mom broke out her rosary and asked us all to pray. Everyone but my dad did. He drank his beer and listened intently to the radio, which was turned low.

I knew at that moment I wanted to be a doctor. No questions asked, no doubt about it, that was it. I was going to be a doctor. I am not a doctor of anything dagnabbit. I did become a paramedic and thoroughly enjoyed that. I hope I was as cool as my mom was during that event. She had no obligation to stop. Had it been up to my dad, we wouldn't have. There was no discussion that I heard about what happened with the little girl as far as injuries. In my mind, she was going to be just fine. My mom had healed all my wounds with somewhat of a strong success record.

My mom also taught me a lot about God and Jesus. I am not a Catholic like she hoped but I am a God-fearing and Jesus-loving man. My mom would pray the rosary every day to and from school. She believed so firmly in the Catholic way and ideology. I knew at around ninth grade that Catholicism was not for me. Too much guilt and hell bound for me to get onboard with that. I knew that hurt my mom a lot. Later on in life, I truly believe my mom was crushed by the church when they took away her rights due to the divorce they refused to absolve. A divorce she did not instigate or ask for.

Overall, my parents made me a bit oval and not well rounded. That is OK though. Everyone needs to have that bit of work they have to do for themselves. My dad was rough and had his strict idea of what a man should be. My mom was a worrier and brought a bit of fear into every aspect of our life. But she was kind and a giver. Both my parents were very principled. You say what you mean, and you stick by your word. Stand up for those who can't stand up for themselves. And know there is always someone greater than yourself.

I am not sure which of my parents pushed education more. I do know that they, and my grandparents, made sure we had the best education. Each of us kids had the opportunity to attend Catholic schools. My older sister went from fourth grade forward, I believe, and my younger sister attended K through 12. Me, I attended fourth through ninth grade. I was not the best student at all. I did decent as far as grades go. I knew my dad would kill me twice if I failed. I tested that theory once or twice and it was true. He did kill me, just FYI.

My teachers were amazing. I told you about a few of my exploits already. I remember my first-grade teacher, Mrs. Cummings. Surprisingly, she also became my fourth-grade teacher. I thought it was cool that I started a new school twice with the same teacher. I remember her very well. I remember how she taught me to write complete sentences. *I will not spit my gum in girls' hair again.* I was supposed to write it 100 times.

Mrs. Cummings was furious at me for multiple reasons. She had got onto me about two hours earlier for putting hard candy in someone's hair. It really was not my fault. I had asthma, which made me prone to a cough. Sometimes that cough expelled any contents of my mouth onto those around me. Oh, I'd cover my mouth, but my hand was so small, and my head moved when I coughed. How could I predict what position my mouth would be in?

I tried to explain my predicament to Mrs. Cummings, but she'd have none of it. Two licks and stern talking did not buy her as much time as she thought. I went back into the classroom and my buddy offered me a Dentyne. I guess the cinnamony spritz that exploded in my mouth resulted in a cough reflex. Next thing I know I hurled that fresh piece of gum directly into Jen's hair. When it came time to the licks, there was not any chat. I got three licks. I then made the fatal mistake of thanking her for taking it easy on me.

That woman became irate. Her nose flared and her face turned red. I made sure to point that out to her by asking her to sit down. She looked like she was going to turn into something I had seen on *Star Trek*. She jerked me by my arm and marched me to the principal's office to call my mom. The call to Mom was a simple courtesy to let her know that I would be staying late as well as let me know I would be beat when I got home.

Anywho, back to the sentence writing. I am not sure when the rest of the world learns to write complete sentences, but I was not an expert at this point in my academic career. The next problem was the number 100. I mean how is a pure-bred southern boy to know how to get from 1 to 100 in first grade. I mean 20 was a stretch on counting abilities (thanks to hide and seek). I was not going to let those obstacles prevent me from getting this job done. I never was much on shying away from a challenge.

I got up there and mimicked every word. Along the way she'd help me number. She taught me that every time I got to the nine just start with the next number and a zero. Easy peasy! The chalkboard held sixty-six sentences. Six rows of eleven sentences. When I had the board full, I turned to Mrs. Cummings and let her know I was at a 100. This was a fact because the board was full. She replied, "No! Erase those and start from sixty-seven."

Chalk-stained paws with little flakes of dust covering my entire body. I had crawled up and down that rolling chair six million times to get to this point. I looked at her dead in the eyes. I said, "No way, Jose," with a chuckle. She got up from her chair making her way towards the eraser. I snagged it as quickly as I could. "You can't Mrs. Cummings." "I can," she replied, "and I will." "NO!!" "Mark, you give me that eraser now." I threw it out the window as far as I could possibly manage.

Oh, she was furious. Once again, we made the march down the hall and out front of the school. She tossed me in the bushes and made me retrieve the eraser like I was a purebred Labrador. Oh, I delayed as much as I could, although she did heave me right upon the eraser. She snatched me by the collar and drug me back to the chalkboard. I refused to write and was beginning to let her know some "what fors" when my mom arrived. Those two had the nerve to double team me.

Knowing what I know now, I had the board 100 percent full, which was a hundred in some sense. I did finish off those thirty-four more sentences, but I did misspell a few words on purpose (I think). After that day I got moved to the front of the class and was monitored for mouth projectiles several times a day. I guess it kept me from getting a nickname that would follow me into the grave. I imagine it would be something like Mark "Spits" Albits.

I have told you about my second-grade teacher, Mrs. Bartese (AKA Mrs. B). Yes, I got my head stuck in a desk and yes, she saved my life. I am sure no one but me remembers that event. Oh, I had Mrs. B so mad at me one day over licks. I tried to explain to her that drilling holes in the board would make it sting more. I told her the principal had his paddle with holes and he sure did pack a wallop. She stated she did not need the holes. I said, "You are right. You're just a girl and you can't hit as hard as a guy." She broke her paddle next time I got licks, which was surprisingly a few minutes later.

I started Catholic school in fourth grade and Mrs. Cummings was in her first year there as well. But fourth grade is where I met my school crush. Her name was Anne and I'll be dagnabbed I can still recall her face. That's a bit of Gordon Lightfeets for ya. But this ain't about Anne and her perfume-scented poetry pen. This is about having the best dern teachers a growing feller could have.

Now, Mrs. Cummings was used to my hijinks and stubborn nature. But what she had not encountered is my profound love and compassion for animals. I sat near the windows that overlooked the playground. I would long to be free of this bondage, frolicking amongst the fields with Anne. Oh, my daydreams were filled with flying high on the swings and telling awesome jokes that would make her smile. She had a great laugh. But we are not talking about her.

One fine day while peering out the windows, I noticed a cat creeping along the large azaleas. This caught my attention as I knew the hunt was on. I watched as the feline stealthily crouched and crawled along the edges of the bushes. I was considering all the things this beast could be tracking. Birds, bunnies, or sasquatch. The more I thought, though, the more my compassion took over. The cat did not look starving. In fact, it was a rather healthy little feline. It was a murderous rabid critter seeking the life of an innocent. It had to be stopped and I was the one to do it.

At that time, I witnessed a happening that would lead to PTSD. This rabid, no good for nothing, feline beast jumped onto an unsuspecting squirrel and latched onto it. I jumped up from my desk yelling, "NO!!!" I ran out the class with Mrs. Cummings in awe and amazement. Stunned by the outburst that broke the serious tensions of a studious environment. Down the hall and out the double doors to the playground I ran. I jumped through the swing and pounced on the rabid beast, retrieving the squirrel from its death grip.

I turned and saw the whole class staring out the window. Mrs. Cummings was slack-jawed and muted from my actions. I wrapped the blood-soaked squirrel up in my nice gray polo shirt (not the name brand, just a collared shirt). I came back to the classroom and sat back at my desk as though nothing ever happened. Of course, people were staring, amazed by the heroic efforts they had just witnessed, I am sure. Everyone was returning to their seats when the principal, Sister Mary Ann, made her entrance into the room.

Apparently, this is something Mrs. Cummings never had encountered before. She called for reinforcements. No one ever knew she left the room. Sister Mary Ann came over to me and snatched me by my ear, leading me to her office. I am certain she was unaware I had a critter wrapped in my shirt. In fact, no one was aware. When we got to her office and I went to sit down, she stopped me mid-seat. "Stand," she said. So, I stood, just holding this poor animal in my hands and shirt.

Sister Mary Ann was on the phone, I thought to call my mom, but apparently, she called Monsignor Hannon. He arrived about five minutes after the call. Still, no one noticed the squirrel I was nurturing to health all the time. The two sat there staring at me when I believe they caught a glimpse of the blood stains on my shirt. "Mark, are you hurt?" "No, Sister." "Well, where did you get all that blood on you?"

I cannot begin to tell you how happy I was when that question was asked. I raised my squirrel friend up with blood dripping from its fresh bite marks. The wounds just happened to be around its nose and mouth. This made the spectacle that much more impactful. They both stood straight up and backed as close to the wall as they could.

"What is that?" was stuttered out with somewhat of a shrill. "Oh, Sister and Monsignor, it is a hurt squirrel attacked by this mean ole cat. I saved it." I let a little tear fall for effect and squeaked my voice some. "Can you help me save its little life?"

Grown-ups just do not know how to handle this situation. They are too tainted by all the worries of life. Rabies, ringworm, missing digits all dance through their frightened minds. Kid, we don't care, we see something hurt and we try to fix it. Barbie doll, mad cow, or sasquatch, we will endeavor to take away the hurtie. My squirrel was hurt, and it needed fixing. I don't remember who got the box for the squirrel, but one appeared. Even some old rags for it to rest. Of course, I was stripped and inspected to ensure that I had no wounds.

My mom was called and notified I would be bringing a friend home. I returned to class with my blood-stained wares, looking like a warrior fresh from battle. I was proud to have taken action. I kept that squirrel at home for about three weeks before it was able to escape the piece-meal cage we had. I had to work extra chores to pay for the shirt I ruined and the extra food the squirrel would need. My dad told me it was to learn more about responsibility.

Two nuns have deeply impacted me. Sister Mary Ann was one of them. I had anger issues when I was young. I remember being so angry at her in the office I yelled at her and said, "God Damn you, Sister Mary Ann." She looked at me and said, "Thank you." I did not know what she meant at the time but later on in life I knew what she meant. I wept when I knew what a snotty little kid said to her out of anger one day.

Sister Rochelle was another nun. Both were at St. Alphonsus when I went there. I do not ever recall saying any cruel things to her. She was so caring and stoic. I did not experience much of that growing up. She wasn't pushing religion on me, but she was showing me genuine love as I imagine Jesus would. When I joined the Navy years later, both Sister Mary Ann and Rochelle would write just to see how I was doing. I was still a punk, but I loved their letters.

Another substantial influence in my life was Jesus. I did not know much about religions and such. I was raised by a devout Catholic mom who still had nude girl photos hanging in the garage and coming in the mail thanks to my dad. I went to church every Sunday and every Friday while in school. I was an altar boy and the whole nine yards. Even thought about being a priest at one time when I was young.

Jesus was a statue in the church to me. I memorized His every feature. So peaceful and kind. Left hand up and right hand over His heart dressed in a long robe draping His entire body. I found myself staring at Him during mass and would swear I would see Him smile directly at me. I would sing as loud as I could just so He could hear me from the front pew. I started my love for Him right there at a very young age.

Even at a young age I knew my pops was not the kind of person I wanted to become. In fact, at this point, there was not any man I knew in real life I wanted to be like. Jesus was the example of a man I wished to become. He stood for something he would not waver from, despite the costs. He was kind and compassionate but stern and fair. He cared for people and did not make promises He could not keep. This was to become my definition of a man and what I tried to live up to.

Like I said, I had anger issues growing up, amongst other things. My mom got me a psychologist, Al. He turned out to be a saving grace in my life. Truly, I do not know where I would be had he not shone his light in my life. Al was funny, not as funny as me though he tried. I was at summer camp before he became my counselor. I was the type of little feller that liked the woods a lot and other kiddos a lot less. We were at the national park, and I was staying away from the pack, more towards the woods.

Al approached me and asked me to come join the group. I was not too nice and told him to get lost, "I do not want to hang out with shitty people!" Al quickly responded, "I am not city, I am country." How can you not laugh at that cheesy comeback? I chuckled. I explained to him I am just not comfortable around that many people. To this day I am not comfortable around loads of people, which means three or more.

Al and I quickly became friends. We would go fishing, canoeing, and just hang out together. It may sound odd, but he was truly a good friend to me. He taught me where my anger came from and a bit on how to control it. He taught me what a pygmy rattlesnake was too. During summer camp he made up this crazy story about a scary old man. He had a mask. One evening when Chuck and I were washing up for dinner, Al snuck down to the bathroom to scare us both. I got so scared I threw my bar of soap and a right cross. Dang, I felt bad because I thought I broke his nose.

I talked to Al up until I got out of the Navy. I got married and just got on with life, I guess. I think about him often. His Camel cigarettes and talking about motorcycles and such. It is a shame to say this, but I don't think I have ever thanked him for all he did for me.

Now I have one more person who greatly influenced me. My PeePaw. Now, you know every pure-bred Southern feller has to mention his peepaw. I am named after my dad's dad, Mark Cleo. I am Mark Charles. My older sister and I are a year and a day apart. When my sister, Victoria, was born my peepaw gave my parents a gift for her and for Mark C. "Next year." A premonition of sorts I would say. At least that is the story I was told.

He and I would sit up and watch Starsky and Hutch, Baretta, John Wayne, and any old western that would come on. He'd get his bowl of butter pee-can Blue Bell® ice cream and I would get a tub of peanut butter. I was/am lactose intolerant, and we were in an airstream. After some cubic feet and highly scientific mathematician calculations we determined peanut butter would be the best for us both.

In the words of Forrest Gump, he and I were like peas and carrots. I just enjoyed being around the guy. One day he bought us a sack of raw oysters. I am highly allergic to shellfish. However, we sat outside the house and shucked a few dozen and I ate a few dozen. My mom came out to get the oysters to fry up and saw me slurp one down. Jiminy pancakes, that woman came undone. She had no words, just the muttering of a possessed demon woman who would kill at any moment. Finally, she screamed out, "Mike!" My dad appeared to a finger pointing at me holding a shell. Oh, my dad belted me and called me retarded and told me I deserve to die.

I vomited later on. My peepaw just laughed at it. He had no idea I was allergic to oysters. It turns out I can eat the little suckers, just not so many. One more story about my peepaw. I was a bigger little feller at this time. I was staying at his place in Cedar Creek, Texas for the summer. He gave me a little job of chopping and stacking chords of wood. One day I was picking up some of the chopped pieces and noticed a little Copperhead snake.

Now, snakes do not scare me at all. But my peepaw had two dogs, one already had been bitten. I made my way in and told him about the snake. He hands me a .38 snub nose. "Hey Peepaw, I never shot a pistol." He says, "It's easy, I'll show you." We walk out to the pile of wood, and I turn over the log to reveal the eighteen-inch copperhead. "Stand back," he says. Bang! Dammit. Bang, bang, Son of a bitch! Bang, bang, bang, mumble, stutter, mumble. I got something for him.

Peepaw hurriedly scrambled inside and appeared holding a .410 shotgun appropriately called the snake charmer. "We'll get him now, Mark C.! Blam! Holy cow, that is a shifty little booger. Reload, blam!" Finally, the would-be assassin was placed out of commission. My peepaw was sweat soaked and breathing heavily. The fight was better than anything I ever saw on the Wide World of Sports. We both sat down later that evening with our ice cream and peanut butter and laughed at that event till our guts hurt and someone farted. I won't say who. Good times with ole Peepaw.

It takes a lot to get a purebred southern born little feller to be a healthy contributor to a society filled with all this noise. I do not think any one of the people who have influenced me will ever be properly thanked. There are no words. I hope my life, with all the imperfections, has somehow been a reflection of them all and their good. I know there are many that I left out, but I hope the pages of my life reveal their impact. My Aunt Mitzie's southern charm and persistence in treating a lady right. My uncles' love of the woods. All my teachers, friends, and passersby. I am a purebred southern-born red, white, and blue-bellied collage of each.

CHAPTER 7

Little feller turns less than little

It is funny when I think about it now. I feel like less of a man than when I was a littler feller. As a pure southern born and bred little feller, manliness was a natural birth effect. I mean was born with the strength of at least 100 of them field oxen. I could bicep curl a small Volkswagen van while chowing down on a cheeseburger. I ate solid food right inside the womb just to be prepared for surviving the world outside. I never crawled a day in my life.

Yep, being a smaller little feller was just so natural. This bigger little feller I have to be today is rough. The path to get here should had made me a natural. I mean I had all the prep any feller could ask for. I still have all my teeth. My ears I believe are the same size I was born with, but I just can't listen with 'em like I used to. I mean to look at me you'd think, *that is definitely a southern born and bred feller of some sorts.*

I guess if I think back far enough, I can remember when

things started to change for me. My dad would travel quite a bit for work. He'd give the usual speech of, "Mark, you are the man of the house now." "Well, of course Pops! Who else can fill these shoes?" I'd puff out my already enormous chest and immediately begin my watch. My pupils would dilate and my parasympathetic nervous system would kick in and I'd shut down that vegetable state. I hated veggies anyhow and when I became man of the house no mom on this planet was gonna get me to eat a green!

At five years of normal peeps age (a ripe ole thirty for southern folks), I manned the house with the helpless three ladies, a few hogs, a Shetland pony, cows, and other farm animals. Every now and then I would slip into my dad's boots to slop the hog bin. However, they were just too small for me. I'd eventually have to put mine back on. I'd carry several five-gallon buckets of water to the critters. Not to show off, I would do them one at a time and sometimes, only towards the end, I'd only fill them up halfway. Like I said, only towards the end.

There was an electric fence all around the field to keep the cows and horse within the perimeter. Lesser men would remember to shut that electric fence off. Not me! I would grab on to that there fence and short it out. I must have blown a hundred fuses in that thing. All one has to do is just stand there long enough and eventually it gives out. The electricity does a lot of the work for the feller. The jaws clench tightly. The legs and foots just become planted right where they is. My body just knew how tough a little feller I was. My hands would just grip that fence tighter and tighter, knowing I was not about to give up.

The fence just warmed me up to the encounters with Budweiser. I was just about to hoof high to ole Bud there. I was easy for him to miss. Understanding this, I had to be soft on him when he stepped on me. That is right, like on me, not just a foot or hand. Bud would just step down and I would be in his stepping path. It was a sad day for him. My head is like a rock, and I twisted his knobby knees a time or two.

The worst thing that beast had done to me though was to poop on me. I mean why, Bud, why? I had the bucket of feed. I had fresh water. I was even going to scratch the rascal's back. It is all my fault. I turned my back on a bull. I remember it so clear and vivid. I bent down to get a handful of hay to lure Anabelle into the barn. I heard the shuffle and thought little of it. The funny thing about cow poo, fresh cow poo, is the weight. You never expect the poo to weigh that much.

The poo struck me on my left shoulder and the wetness of it ran straight through to the crack of my hiney. Each plop of the manure drove me to the ground. I literally fell over. The steaming mess of gnawed plant-based plant food covered every square inch of my muscled-up back. I was toned for a five-year-old. Most fellers and fellets would have been a bit grossed out by this. Not this little feller. I was mad. I got up and knocked ole Bud right upside the head. He just stared at me.

Now, don't feel bad for ole Bud. He managed to step on me a few times, kick me numerous times, and drool gallons of slobber across various parts of me. All of which were forms of payback, I am certain. Bud was not the most vicious ani-mule we had. You may not believe this, but the most foul, ornery, and mean-spirited critter we had was the rooster. I am sure that the ole rooster was Satan spawned.

I would come in there with chicken feed in tow. Maybe even some ole cracked shell for a treat. Innocent as a newborn northern babe (us southern babes may not be so innocent). I would scan my peepers around the assembly of hens, ensuring I found that nasty beast of a bird. DO NOT ENTER the cage without at least one peeper dialed into his whereabouts. He is sneaky and conniving. Just waiting to sink those avian poo–infested talons deep inside my flesh.

This bird had to be of Russian decent. He would rush in and plant those spurs and rush back to realign. One day I had lost focus. This day was coming for the both of us though. A reckoning of sorts. I made my way with said feed in hand. Fresh water lay in the wait. Hens a-pecking away at the strewn-out feed. Content, dare I say happy, with the challenge of scarfing down the new vittles politely provided by this statue of a little feller.

The bucket of feed was on its way to empty. I could feel the gate latch in my hand. That is when the feud began. The ole devil rooster himself slammed his spur into my right calf. He let out a screech, I assume from the pain he felt from penetrating a real man's flesh. I winced, gritted my teeth, and set up to form a well-placed kick. Before I could get myself properly planted, the beast struck again. Striking an artery this time as blood spewed forth from my gaping wound somewhere yet to be determined on my body. The rooster was getting cocky now. Bobbing his head and clucking as we circled, eyes locked.

I swear that rooster was trembling. His steps were calculated, but so were mine. I was ready this time. He lined up for the attack. I did my best Bruce Lee karate chop/kick straight to the eyeball of the rooster. We both did a rolling recovery. I grabbed his beady little throat. He gouged my forearms and chest trying to get my eyes. Two, no three, punches to the head and a swift uppercut. He's had enough surely. The beast was right. Sadly, I had no more. I loosened my grip, and the bird staggered a bit and then fell.

We both were panting heavily. I was bleeding more externally. I convinced myself that his injuries were internal. I laid on the chicken poop–covered ground trying not to show the obvious signs of blood loss. The amazement in the ole rooster's eyes was very similar to mine. As we stared at each other, the hens pecked the ground clean. I worked my way to a standing slumped position. Collected my wares and limped towards the gate without breaking eye contact. The rooster just watched as I made my way out. I won't say this was our last tussle or our worst, we both were measured though.

I am thankful for being the man of the mini-farm those many times ole pops travelled. I tell you one must be tough and cunning to be proficient at manliness in the southern hemisphere. Dealing with my sisters was an even tougher task. Those two were slyer than the ole rooster even if they were not as mean spirited. My older sister, Victoria, had put the aforementioned eye drops into my eyes. I never recovered from that blindness she caused.

There was no need to try to have healthy discussions with Vicki about me being the man of the house and all. She was too clever and used a lot of words I just could not understand. I believe it was a foreign language of ancient times. She was possessed too. Come to think about it now, we must have lived on an ancient Indian burial site.

Now, my sister plotted. When my dad was home, she would cause some catastrophic incident that would leave me incapacitated and unable to perform my manly duties. Or so she thought. For the consideration of all ye readers. She and I were doing dishes one day. Knowing I had to use the dishwasher door to achieve the appropriate height to put away said cleaned dish, she opened the cabinet door. My head thusly, for to wit, struck the cabinet door, splitting the door and my head.

I ran to the bathroom, where I was met by two very angry parents. One screaming how could I damage the cabinet, the other why did I step on the dishwasher door. The blood was less than what I expected for a head wound. I mean it only saturated a full roll of toilet paper, two full size towels, and filled the tub half full. Oh, I feel lightheaded. Needless to say, I was in serious trouble for the damage. Vicki just sort of snickered, at least in my mind. All this to keep me from achieving the manliness of the house.

Kristi was a breeze compared to everything else. I was sort of a hero to my little sister. She looked up to this ole southern feller. In fact, she was my pal. No joke. Why she liked me, I had no idea. I was a true-blue brother pain in the rumpkus. I shot her with my BB gun. I thought it was empty. I felt bad. I don't remember if I laughed though. Maybe I did? You talk about injuries, though. This poor girl.

I mentioned the pitchfork earlier that she drove through her foot after a hurricane. She also pert near took her toe off with a shovel during a pool construction incident. The one event that sticks with me in my nightmares is the picnic bench seat falling on her ankle. Goodness, what an event. My dad built this picnic bench to drive eighteen-wheelers on. It was heavy and stout. It took the neighborhood to move just a seat. It was probably 20 million feet long and weighed at least seventy metric tons.

One day we were out setting up for a feast, I am sure. Kristi climbed the behemoth and then the seat just rolled somehow. She fell back and to the ground. The seat followed the path of gravity, choosing a soft landing on her ankle instead of the cold concrete. The scream and wail scared us all. We knew it was a lost limb for sure. Pops pulled the seat back with all his might. Mom pulled Kristi from the clench of the seat.

We all gasped for a moment, but everything was there. It was amazing how quickly everyone went into action. Ice, car keys, towels, and off to the emergency room. Kristi would return that evening. No cast or missing feet. See, them southern gals, they are pretty tough too. They have to be. I take a lot of credit for how tough Kristi is. I gave her a lot of grief, as a southern brother should, but she obviously was the better for it. I am glad she did not test my manliness duties with injuries like that on my watch. Come to think of it, I may have been better at this manliness than pops.

My dad had laid out some manliness criteria for me. Men are tough. Check! Men drink beer. Blick! Men don't cry. Wait. What? I am truly a little feller man of men. No doubt. I cry though. I tell you when ole Sambo died, I bawled. It was a tragedy and the tears flowed. When Jaclyn Smith got hurt while I watched the *Charlie's Angels*, I shed a tear or two. I cried when John Wayne died in *The Shootist*.

All those were purposeful tears. Mainly for respect. I did not have to cry. I did it because I wanted to. To prove it to my pops, I let him beat me senseless daily with no more than a "bring it on, old man." Apparently, that is when tears help. A little feller is supposed to relent a bit when an older feller is beating them. There is a system for these things and tears and begging should be applied about the third or fourth crack of the belt.

I was just not built that way. I was brought into this ole world on the first day of spring in the sweltering humid air of South Mississippi. I immediately had to thicken the ole veneer. I always felt I had the advantage when pops went to whipping. He would hold me by one arm and beat me with the other. Keep in mind he was a drinker. SO ... I would just start running in a circular pattern. A spin one or two times and he'd wear out, get dizzy, and quit. At the very least he'd lighten up a tad.

The one thing I learned early on is never put your free hand behind you to block the blow. No way, no how. Your best bet as a little feller who was foreordained for a life of whippings was proper pants. See, when you go to the TG&Y or Kmart for pants, do not get fancy. No sir or ma'am. You find the jeans that are the toughest, thickest, and stiffest jeans you can find. In my opinion it was Rustlers. I could not help that they had a cool name.

Rustlers were so stiff and thick they bent you when you tried to walk in them. You will be thankful when the belt beatings begin. I have seen sparks fly as those jeans deflected blow after blow from that length of leather being propelled at my hiney. Rustler jeans have saved me on many occasions. Selflessly enduring the abuses meant solely for my backend. It was enduring all this simply due to my misdeeds. The times I fell from my bike doing well over the speed of light, they saved me from scrapes and bruises. They saved me from the beatings for getting the very jeans dirty during that wreck and were now standing between my flesh and the forty lashes.

They are the secret to how a little feller won't shed a tear when the reign of fury is expelled onto their backside. Yet will cry out loud when Mom throws their favorite pair of jeans away. A little feller hated growing spurts just because their dear friends would be laid to rest in a rag bin. The best one could hope for is to pass it on to the Salvation Army for another little feller to use. Already broken in and well versed in the protection clauses required for all little fellers everywhere.

You are right, I did not elaborate on not liking beer. To this day I probably have one to two beers a year. I am not a drinker. I spent four years in the Navy and was drunk twice in those four years. My whole life, all fifty-three years to this point, I probably consumed greater than my limit a dozen times. I never acquired the taste for it.

I do remember the first time a little feller was offered a beer by a bigger feller. I was helping my Uncle Joe, Uncle Pete, and Grandpa Manieri put up a fence. We had cleared the forty-acre plot and were digging post holes. I was in charge of dragging the post over to the dug holes. They were creosote post, which I later found out will burn the snot out of lesser fellers, but I was fortunate, I only got second-degree burns. Others would have simply perished right there on the spot.

Now we had been at this most of the day. My uncles had kept little ponies (beer) in the cooler along with Cokes. I liked to drink from the spigot we had out there, but an ole bottle Coke was a treat to be had. I was also in charge of getting whatever the grown folks needed for drinks or whatnot. On one trip to the cooler, my Uncle Joe made the request for three beers and "grab yourself one too." I was like, *great; I am finally recognized as a bigger little feller here now.*

I arrived at the meeting place with four beers in tow. I fully expected them to say, "What are you doing?" However, no one batted an eye. I ran into my first hurdle early on. Twisting the top off these rascals was tough. There was definitely some intrusion-proofing placed on the cap. I guess this was to keep the women folk with delicate little hands from trying to open the man's drink. My mitts were tough as the leather gloves I was wearing.

The tops were persistent too. I twisted and pulled, and it just slipped around in my paws. I watched my uncles. A quick twist and pop, they were guzzling down the delightful nectar. Grandpa used the same method. Twist, swoosh of air, cloud of delight and guzzle. I turned my back so they would not see my focus. Twist, daggnabbit, twist, twist. Grip, twist, grunt, fart, and finally it yielded to my persistence. Ha! It was open! I sniffed the open golden juice. Nothing the other fellers had done, and I see why. It smelled horrid. My feet did not smell like that after an all-day stomp fest.

I propped that tiny bottle of beer and started to guzzle. Oh, my goodness. Choke, gag, spit, spit, spit. I heard the yelling but was just trying to survive the poisoning I was sure I was given. "Uncle Joe, this one must be bad. It tastes like ole socks." I know how old socks taste, thanks to Joey B. in third grade. Uncle Joe said, "Nah, that is how beer taste ,son, you'll get used to it." I thought to myself there is no way. But once you start something you have to finish it. That is part of the man thing us fellers have to endure. I finished that rascal barely and then drank a gallon of water to expel the demonic taste in my mouth.

Becoming a man is a series of events that I reckon happen over a lifetime. I am still really not comfortable stating

I am a full-grown man these days. I am a man biologically speaking but a real man, eh, maybe two-thirds there. I am not a Navy SEAL kind of feller. Now, there is a MAN. I don't know how it happens really. When I was a littler feller, I had less to worry with and could speak my mind freely. They just chalked it up to my wee-sized underdeveloped brain. They still could today, but the body tells a story that would deem a butt-kicking more appropriate.

Now, I remember the change within my body. I woke up one day and things were different. No, that came up before I woke up, way before I went through this. That day I woke with a hair. A long, black curly hair. Just one. I was like, why did this happen? I shrugged it off and yanked the lone defect out. I went to school and thought about Anne all day. That was normal too. I was going to marry Anne since the fourth grade, now I was almost in sixth grade. The very next morning I woke up and checked things out. I now had sprouts under my arms as well as in the nether regions. MOOOOOOOMMMMMMM!!! I needed my mom to tell me what form of beast I have been bitten by to leave me in this state. I was thinking werewolf diseases or some sort of rabies variant. Was I becoming a sasquatch?

"Wait, Mom, what do you mean this is a normal process of life?" I had been doing just fine without any additions to my body for multiple years now. Better than a decade almost. Why did I need more hair? *Look at my head and eyebrows. I don't even need that hair.* "Make it stop, Mommy! Make it stop." Mom rushed out of the room and did the thing I absolutely did not want her to do. "Mike, you need to talk to Mark about the puberty changes." *Ugghhh. Why him?*

Luckily, it was a quick conversation.

"Son, do you like girls?"

"Yes, I do, Pops."

"You do!? The GI Joe dolls threw me."

"Oh brother!"

"Well, you're about to start to like them more."

"I am going to marry Anne."

"No, you are not, she is smart and above your capabilities. Do they teach you to read in that school you attend?"

"Yes, sir."

He threw down a book on the bed. *Doctors Talk to 9 to 12-Year-Olds.* Dang, I got to read about this junk too. Dad finished off about smacking some little nibblet off in the house and how it won't happen without me losing it. I just agreed in a puzzled tone. The book was not much help. Hair is just going to happen. I went from little feller to little man sometime between being man of the house on interim basis and hairy pits.

It is funny how moms are. She bought me deodorant and smelling-good stuff. There was not any instruction with the products provided. I smeared the deodorant all over without prejudice. Brut 33 splashed upon all my body parts. I tolerated the burning and thought it was part of the man experience. I stepped out of that bathroom all manned up and immediately there were responses. I was recognized as a man, I thought. I was stopped by my mom with the question/concerned tone of ,"How much did you use?"

"The whole thing, Mom."

"Which did you use the whole thing of?"

"The spray stuff and the liquid stuff. I put it all over."

"Go shower and I will have your dad talk to you about how to put that stuff on."

You know, the funny thing about using that amount of smell goodness, it does not want to come off despite how much Dial soap you use. Pops never did have that talk with me. I did overhear him tell Mom that he fully expected me to drink the smell-good products. I never did tell them that I did gurgle a bit of it.

Becoming a man is difficult at best for most other fellers. Us pure bred southern fellers, well, we just are naturals at it. Part of manhood enterness is the ability to handle weaponry of all sorts. My first weapon, mud-bombs, were made specifically from crawdaddy mounds. See, that ole craw-pops would take the mud from their housing and stack it outside. I believe they like the feeling of living in castles with those big mud stacks.

The trick to utilizing mud-bombs effectively is size management. You cannot have the bomb too big because it limits launch and ballistic capabilities. Now, I know you are thinking that me being a pure born and bred southern little feller entering man feller status, I would be able to launch at least a full-size F150. I could! Maybe three times, five at tops. Mud-bombs have to be delivered in a frenzy with enough quantity to ensure limited advancement by the enemy. As everyone realizes size matters, and too small, oh, I shudder to even think. Small mud-bombs never prevented them enemies from taking over.

The neighborhood gang would engage in combatives pretty much weekly. We'd make our trenches and barricades. We would meticulously gather our mud-bombs (apologizing to the craw-critters for the castle theft). We would study our enemy and discuss our past encounters to ensure a successful engagement. We'd count down from twenty and about three we'd begin our lobbing. No, not to cheat. Solely for the element of surprise.

The mud-bombs would rain down upon us with fury. Our return fire was spontaneous and calculated. Out of nowhere a flank maneuver catches Pete in the side and he's injured. I lob two, maybe three bombs in left flank's direction. I attempt to pull Pete to recovery, but dang he is heavy. Mud-bombs are landing all around me. Heart beats way faster than an Indian motorcycle. Pete whispers, "Just leave me." No! I unload the fifty or so mud-bombs I have on me. There is a lull in the action, and I get Pete on his feet, and we run to our next station. DO NOT EVEN THINK RETREAT. Shame on you. We don't retreat. We regroup.

We get to the next station. Pete and I are looking over our stash. We assess our wounds and contemplate our next move. All of a sudden, I heard this beast of a howl. I feel the sting of the mud bomb barrage and pelt every inch of my body. I see the blackness of death fall upon me as I hit the solemn, hallowed ground that was to be my final resting place. A few more close-range impacts and the sound of laughter. I cannot believe my ears of whose voice I heard in the celebratory sounds. *Is that Pete? What the hay? No, never?*

Sure enough. Pete had been a mole. He was paid off in the form of kisses and womanly attention, I am sure. Oh, we were playing against Tina and Liz, by the way. I know, I know. I should have seen the possibility of traitorship. The savory smell of victory let my judgement get clouded. It was a sad defeat for sure. Luckily, I was woken up by the fire ants eating my flesh from bones. Mud bombs leave some serious bruises, but nothing as deep as a fellow feller selling one out for kisses and tricked by the wiles of a fellet. Come to think of it, I guess fellets learn of weapons mastery too. Theirs is much more sophisticated and highly accurate, however.

Luckily, we moved on and got past that betrayal. Pete and I are still good friends to this day. I won't go to war with him, but he is a friend, nonetheless. That reminds me, he was supposed to join the Navy with me and recanted on that. HMMM?

Speaking of fellets. I feel that is sort of part of becoming a man in a feller's life. No, I am not going to tell you about intimate details of datingship. That is just gross, frankly. However, I have mentioned Anne Marie several times here. She is my first crush, maybe even love. I mean I dreamt of marriage and kiddos and growing old with her. We talked a lot on the phone and in school. What does this have to do with a lil feller becoming a man? Rejection!

See, a man must know how to take rejection, well, like a man. There can't be any of that crying or contemplating the what ifs. No man begs for what he wants if he doesn't get it. Maybe food, he'll beg for food, I mean being hungry sucks. But on the whole, no begging. My rejection came early. Way before Anne crushed my tiny anvil of a ticker. I mean Theresa, our babysitter, was probably twenty years older than me. Simply a dream. Told me I was a grubby dirty little troll when I asked her to be my girlfriend. I was five.

Jaclyn Smith never once returned any of the letters I sent. I am not talking emails either. I am talking handwritten, stamped, and mailed letters. Those letters would cost me a whole weekend of mowing the yard and trimming. The trimmers we had were scissor types and we lived on three acres. Whether she realizes it or not, she and my pillow made me the heck of a great kisser I am today. So, yes, by the time I got to the devasting rejection by Anne in the eighth grade, I was hardened to the brink of manliness already. I barely remember the event, but maybe I can get the details out of my brain and onto this parchment.

It was the eighth-grade year. I had practiced all summer long with the junior varsity football team. I sucked at football but was happy to be on the team. It was long days of running and weights, which I loved. Every now and then the cheer team would be at the school, practicing their routines. Anne was on the cheer team. No other students were at the school besides the football team and occasionally the cheer team. Well, the brothers and nuns were there. Remember, I went to catholic school.

I blame the event all on Coach Earnie. He made a big

deal of how I looked good in pads. I made plans, the next day was to be our first full pads practice. Those practices were short, only about half a day. I knew the cheer team would be onsite due to some covert intel sharing. (Thanks, Erin.) I asked my mom if Anne said yes, would she take us to the movies. Mom gushed about the possible upcoming date and stated that she was not a taxi service, find another ride. So, I would steal a car, I decided. Anne was going to be my forever girlfriend. No expenses spared.

I was walking out to practice, and I saw the cheer team congregating at the edge of the field. They were talking of tumbles, cheer chants, and boy tactics. I said, "Hey Anne!" I know it's clever the way I was not letting on to my extreme excitement about our lives merging to oneness. Small talk ensued. How's your day, you ready for school to start, yadda, yadda. "You sure look nice, Anne."

"Aw, you're always sweet."

"Hey, would you want to go to the movies on a date? I'd steal a car to take you since my mom won't drive me."

"I would NEVER, EVER, EVER date you! Ew!" She literally gagged. Her voice was loud enough for the entire state of South Mississippi (that is correct, South Mississippi is a state in and of itself) to hear. She turned, head down, and stomping her mumbling something that sounded like … humiliated.

I shrugged, having gave it my best, and proceeded to begin practice. This is where the man part comes in. Everyone, including coach Earnie, laughed. Not a chuckle laugh either. No. I am talking full belly laughs. Al (that's what they called me), what makes you think a beautiful woman like her would ever go out with you? In fact, what makes you think any woman would? The cashier at the Popeyes laughed at me after practice when I went to get my spicy dark three-piece special. They laughed so hard I did not get my biscuit and only two pieces of regular chicken. I was served legs, fellers. Legs only!!!! You surely have to be a man to endure this.

School started a week or two later. I thought the sting was over. Brother Charles pulled me aside after computer lit. and stated he and the dean wanted to chat. I was like oh brother, did they really know about me not flushing the toilet when I had diarrhea this morning? When I arrived at the dean's office there was the dean, a counselor, Brother Charles, and an unknown priest.

"Mark, we'd like to talk with you about the event that has taken place."

"Look, I have IBS or some bowel issues, I get diarrhea, sometimes I can't control it. Look in my locker and you'll find extra trousers and underwear. I swear I can't control it."

"Uh-humm. No, Mark, that is not what we are talking about. The other event that happened."

"Are you talking about when I peed in the student parking lot?"

"No! The event where you asked Anne Marie out and she politely declined to acquiesce your request. We brought in a counselor because you must be crazy to think a girl of that caliber would ever consider going out in public with you."

"Well, thank you all, but I already have a counselor, Al,

and he totally agrees I am crazy. It is OK though because I am not crazy enough to need special ed. Yet!"

It is funny the concern and the looks you get for asking a popular girl out. Anne was, and maybe is, out of my league. Aren't most women. One never knows though, until you try. Yes, it did sting quite a bit. My affections for Anne never wavered. I saw her profile on LinkedIn the other day and my heart skipped a little. That may be my cardiac condition. Anne was special as she was my first love and my first heartache without even so much as a date.

Other heartaches have came and went. Some I have endured with every bit of manliness one could possibly imagine. Others, I acted way worse than any little feller should or ought to. It strikes me curious as to how rejections occur almost every day. They are our most overlooked part of going from little feller or fellet to bigger fellers and fellets. Those circumstances help mold our character and ensure that we get better. There was nothing wrong with me asking Anne or Anne saying no. We did not explode or die due to the event. We both did learn from it though.

Going from a lil feller to a man is still a mystery to me. I definitely do not remember any specific moment in time when the transition occurred. I have fought too many fights. I have cried a lot of tears. Not too much beer and booze. I have been through a war. Seen death and births. Good times and bad. Not sure if that helps with the manliness or not. In my mind I am just a lil feller, trying to keep up with all those bigger fellers.

CHAPTER 8

The Cul-de-Sac of Memory Lane

There is so much I remember. I could fill these pages a hundred times over with all the snippets that jump into my mind. Some things I wish I could forget like the day Sambo died or the day the towers fell. There are many memories I cling to and cherish. I hope my memory vault stays accessible as the miles continue to rack up. Unfortunately, I cannot find my keys and wallet most days. I leave them in the same place every day too.

Time never allows us to truly enjoy the moments or soak them in. As our lives unfold, those moments are imprinted on our hard drives. Some things we never intended as a memory stay with us forever. The sound of thunder echoing off the water. The sound of belt swiftly being extracted from Pop's blue jeans. Some things we try to remember, we forget. The way we felt when we first tasted liverwurst and grape jelly. We know it is good and that is all.

Growing up in South Mississippi is a privilege and

a blessing. I can remember the way the grass smelled on those hot, humid afternoons. I could lay in the woods and soak up the smells. Man, the peace one could get there is indescribable. The red bugs and ticks one could get are also unforgettable. My poor mom has seen my genitals more times than a mom should ever have too. I'd run into the living room shorts pulled down to my ankles. Red whelps all over my little cherries and hiney. She would always give me a difficult time.

"Mark, did you put your winky where it don't belong?"

"No, Mom, I was out in the woods!"

"Naked?"

I couldn't lie, sometimes I was just frolicking naked through the woods or skinny dipping in the bayou and cold spring steams.

Mom was not gentle about the tick removals either. She would snatch them suckers off by hooking up her Pinto to the critter and flooring it. I would cling to an ole pine for dear life. Flesh and bones would rip away along with the monstrosity of a being once attached. I had a big grey tick attached to me once. It was so big I had anemia for seventy-two years and lost eighteen pounds after its removal. Oh, the sweet memories.

The smell of rain hitting the asphalt brings back memories of playing in the ditch during and after rains. We'd swim in them or at least waller around. The current would rip down from one end of the street to the other. We'd try to make anything float from my sister's Barbie to Jess's bike. Once we even tried to get Pete's go-cart to float. Once we had our riding mobiles (AKA bikes), we'd trek along the ditch byways slinging mud, grass, and tears. We were practically Hell's Angels of the ditch.

We would construct ramps out of any ole thing we could. The faster the current and the wider the ditch, the more determination to fly across it. We would calculate the required angular momentum and parallel universe constructs to ensure speed and ramp degrees were appropriate. The girls did most of that math stuff. Remember, fellers and fellets, school is highly important. We set everything according to the calculations. Pete was the first up because, well, Pete always goes first.

He took off. There was still a slight bit of rain falling and the occasional crack of thunder in the distance. The cicadas, frogs, and tadpoles were silenced by the anxiety in the air. The doves whispered, ooooo, in the background. One more deep breath and Pete was off. The banana seat swaying back and forth with each quadricep-driven crank of the pedal. Pete made it to the desired speed of 3,888 mph just as he hit the ramp. Swish, silence, and ka-thunk. One successful landing but just a tad short.

I checked the air in my tires. I pressed the front hand brake to ensure engagement. I peered over the mighty river raging out in front of me. The miles of ramp laid out just for me to jump into stardom. I heard the calls from Evel Knievel and the Bionic Man playing in my head. I knew ole Jaclyn Smith would be waiting on the other side of the river. I rocked my bike back and forth before my final shove off.

The rain was falling harder, and lightning was twirling all about. Hurricane force winds were attacking me head on. I pedaled harder. I was not doing this for myself any longer. No! It was for the ladies who needed a hero, the children all around who needed something to believe in, I was doing this for the grand ole State of Southern Mississippi and the good ole USA. I hit the base of the ramp a pert near perfect speed. I felt the front tire clear the ramp as I took flight. Ten feet, fifteen feet, two hundred feet I watched as I effortlessly cleared the river below. I could not be more proud of the ole bike.

Now what I failed to realize beforehand, but it became so glaringly obvious, was the fact that I did not tighten that front tire. It apparently got tired right before landing and let loose. The forks dug into the side of the ditch hurling me chest and shoulder first across the asphalt street. Don't worry though. The asphalt had these perfectly placed white shells embedded, perfectly exposed, just to slow my momentum to a grating stop.

The only thing one can do at this point is jump up like nothing happened. The rain made the bleeding look worse than it was. I was not breathing at this point since the contact with the ground somehow stole all the air my lungs had to offer. I heard Pete say he could see my chin bone and honestly, I could not move my arms to try and check it out. What would Knievel do in this situation? I could only muster a grimace. Tina tore the remainder of shirt off me as she vomited from the site of the damage. My sisters ran and told Mom and Pops. Dad beat me, Pete laughed, and

Mom expressed her concerns over the damaged clothes. I survived, in case anyone was wondering.

Yep, it is amazing what memories are stored up there in this old noggin. I remember my mom sitting on our couch drinking her Cold Duck and eating her popcorn. She never looked particularly happy or sad. I just think she was content. Watching M.A.S.H. or some other series of Dad's choosing. Dad would always be in his recliner when he was home and not playing pool. He would drink his Manhattans with or without the beer chaser. He was a drinker. I never saw him as a happy man either. He seemed mad most of the time. I am sure I influenced that mood and probably those drinks more than I realized.

Every night before bed, we'd kiss Mom good night. My sisters would hug my dad. I was left to a handshake because men don't hug other men. Of course, I fail at that not hugging rule today as well. I came to fear, then dread those handshakes. They were not meant as affection or respect. They were downright painful. He loved to squeeze the bageezums out of my paws. Goodness, my hands ache right now just thinking of it. In retrospect, it was just his way of seeing how tough I was. Maybe this is one of those times I should have squealed a bit more.

Sundays after church we would head to Bay St. Louis to our grandparents' place. We simply referred to it as "the country." Thousands of acres for a little feller to get lost and get away from everyone. I already mentioned my aunts and uncles. A bunch of Sicilian descendants eating and drinking. Waving hands and telling all kinds of stories.

Me, I headed into the woods. They had these baboo cane patches where I would select the correct rod for the day. I'd have some form of string and I could make a hook from a branch. I would whittle it down to a point on each end with my trusty ole knife.

Worms were easy to find. Drive a good-sized stick into the ground and run your knife blade across the top. The vibrations would send the worms up. One has to be selective about where to drive the stick, but for the most part, worms are everywhere. They fit great into a pocket. Sam, whenever he was alive, would be my partner, but most of the time I was alone. Like ole Huck Finn.

I could fish for hours. I could be by myself for hours, no problem. I am still very much at peace on my own. I have seen deer, turkey, squirrel, rabbit, and all sorts of wildlife along the creek banks. I did not have any ATV or motor bikes at that time, so I walked the million or so miles through the logging trails. I would dream about the Indians that occupied the area prior to my grandma's family's arrival. I think it was the Biloxi Indians that was local to the area. There were a few Indian graves in the graveyard on the land.

One of my favorite stories my Great-Uncle Dolphie would tell is about him and his brother, Toby, hog hunting with the Indians. Toby had shot a big ole hog and was so proud of it. The Indians had cut down a sapling tree and tied the hog up to carry it out. Somewhere in transit that ole hog revived itself and came a-loose from its bindings. Toby and Dolphie were startled from the commotion and frozen in their tracks for a minute. When they began to look around, not a single Indian was in sight. They had shimmied up the trees as quick as a possum. Toby and Dolphie followed suit, leaving the hog to its retreat.

There was not a tribe of Indians at that time. I understood it to be just a handful. It is crazy to think how Dolphie remembered his childhood and would share it with me. He told me some of his stories a hundred times over. He went to a schoolhouse that taught all ages in one sitting. The first naked girl he seen was in that schoolhouse. She got in trouble during class and the teacher had her drop her pants in front of the class to receive her spanking. This happened to the boys as well. But everyone was shocked in class because gals are not common troublemakers in the south. They are debutantes and therefore seen as the example of proper. Very much the opposite for a southern feller. We are not so much the example of proper, but we do set the standard for manliness and what all fathers fear their daughters ending up with.

I have two great friends I have known for the better part of my life. You know how Pete and I became friends. It started off with him beating the tar out of me and eventually pity took over and the friendship spurned from there. Wait, I meant spawned from there. My other friend is Danny. I met him in first grade at St. Martin. It was a little different from Pete's friendship development. Danny just hated me to start off. He did not beat me senseless, although I know for a fact there were multiple times he wanted to kill me, and he could.

Now there is an unknown, known etiquette when there is that much pure-bred, true-blue, southern born-ness in one location such as a school or even a saloon. If a feller wants to join the clan, he can't just step into the circle. No ma'am or sir. A feller must linger on the fray in an unsuspicious yet obvious manner. That is where I excelled at. I was always the peeper trying to peep my way into a friendship of sorts. Now don't go a-thinking that I actually needed friends. Far from it. Folks needed me in their lives, whether they knew it or not.

I hung on the outskirts of Danny's tribe. During lunch they would try to move table to table, but I would just pack up my braunschweiger and grape jelly sandwich, and silently move over to a table close by. At recess, I would have my usual bowl break and then seek out where the crowd was hanging at. As a side note, I think I had IBS. I could not hold anything longer than ten minutes after ingestion. In class, I sat a row over just as not to impose.

Now, where some would say I was a bit intrusive but I would say I was a power player, was when I visited Danny's house. Mind you, he did not live down the street. I had to travel about two miles to his house on my sister's ten-speed. Down Kruger place, past Nix Road, onto Old Fort Bayou. All two-lane traffic. My parents strictly forbade this type of travel as it was not a heavily traveled road but it was a main road. They did not realize that I could do 95 mph in tenth gear, so getting run over was not even a concern.

The trick was getting down Old Fort Bayou Road undetected. See, if my mom or pops caught me, they'd run me over. The trips would involve some stealthy maneuvering. I would lay down in the ditches, hide behind street signs, and occasionally camouflage myself with various twigs and foliage. Becoming one's friend is not a task to be taken lightly. All measures should be taken to ensure success. After all, friends are for life!

I would just show up out of the blue and knock on the door. Mrs. Pat, Danny's mom, would inevitably open the door. She was sometimes shocked by the state of my appearance. Most of the time Danny was out, occasionally he was there with a sincere look of disdain on his face. I know it is difficult for fellers to just let out their true feelings, so I just hung out with little to nothing said. Every now and then he would take me for a ride on his three-wheeler ATV or CB 125 motorcycle. Mostly though it was five to ten minutes of silence and then I would make my trek back home.

I never had any fancy moochinery like three-wheeled rockets or knobbed-up power bikes. NO! I did have a 3-million-donkey-powered lawn tractor vehicle. OK, it was my dad's lawn tractor. That I used without his permission 99.99999 percent of the time. Yes, yes you can say I stole it. I was a nasty little southern born and bred thief of a feller. Not too proud of it at all, but I would have been too perfect otherwise. I have to have some flaws.

Now, the things I could do with this all-terrain-tractor was amazing. I did it solely to keep up with Danny and Pete on their off-road adventures. I needed friends. They were simply riding for fun. Me, I was traveling out of desperation, and some fear. I had to ride like this was my last day on earth, because when Pops found out it could very well be.

I believe top speed on that rascal was 237.88 mph. I would crank it full throttle. This machine had cruise control, whereas Danny and Pete's simply had hand controls they had to maintain. I remember my first obstacle, besides the hot wiring, was a raging river. I watched Danny cutting donuts and running up the steep embankments with his ATV. I had to try this. Down the side I went, across the seventy-feet deep water. Their eyes were glued on me, and why not. I was amazing.

The water rose above the steering device and about chest high. The tractor pressed on resiliently in the face of the treacherous adversity that lay out in the rapids. Wheels were digging into sloppy earth beneath them. I saw craw-daddies and other crustaceans kicking up in our wake. We approached the other side and began our ascent out of the raging river. All kinds of vegetation had clung to the lawn machine attempting to prevent it from reaching its goal. We crested the peak to find Danny and Pete waiting on the other side.

"What the heck, maaaannnnn?" Danny asked.

Pete stated the obvious. "Your dad is going to kill you when he finds out!"

"Oh, come on. How is he ever going to know?" I replied fully understanding that dads all around the world are built to detect these types of shenanigans.

I rolled over hills and down through the bayous. That tractor just kept on putting out. Sure, I had to get off and push it through several mud bogs, but the cruise control made it simple enough. I got home and hosed it off, replaced the deck, and parked it back in the garage all before Pops got home. About 9:30 p.m. I was snatched out of bed by the arm of Hercules.

"Did you take my tractor for a little joy ride today?" Pops thundered out waking the entire southern hemisphere.

I could not hide the smile as I remarked, "Yes!"

Oh, the shades of color that man's face went through before the pounding began. I knew he was seriously mad, because he was speaking in tongues and broken sentences. Listen, by this time I was a pro at paying the consequences in spades for my wild spirit. It ain't easy being a pure born and bred southern feller with a need for speed and no pocketbook to support it. I believe that it may have been tough on a lot of bystanders.

Danny and Pete still talk about my antics with the lawnmower. There is not one person in Gil's bar that hasn't heard the stories from Danny. All wives, children, and girlfriends have heard those stories. I believe those two told my Navy recruiter and several potential bosses. I don't blame them, I was amazing on that two-wheel-drive all-terrain machine.

It really wasn't until high school that Danny and I actually hung out on purpose. Our relationship was rocky at best. We both had old trucks our paps let us borrow on occasion. We would take full advantage of that by running the heck of those mobiles. We would race up and down the roads. To be honest, Danny is a way better driver than I am. He could sling that truck around the curves on Deisel Road, which was a dirt road behind the high school, like it weren't nothing. That truck was completely sideways most of the time, yet we'd travel straight down the road.

I kid you not, Danny had skill when it came to driving. He really missed out on being a professional driver of any sort. Me, I was not even considered a driver. My driver's ed teacher simply passed me to meet the quota. I desperately tried to keep on par with Danny. Once we had ventured down Diesel Road. He in his truck and me in mine (well, our paps'). I couldn't sling the truck around the curves like Danny, so he stayed well ahead of me. We come to the end of Deisel Road to a location called Blue Lake.

Blue Lake was surrounded by a dirt portion and some gravel. Danny had parked his truck and was waiting for me to arrive. This is how I know we were friends at this point. I came charging in there with all 1,000 HPs a-flowing and foot in the radiator. I wanted to show him how good a poor driver I was. At the last minute I cut that wheel to the left and the back slung around right through a mud hole. The mud hole was perfectly aligned with Danny's rolled-down winder. Due to my momentum and circular velocity, the mud hole propelled its contents directly into the cab of the truck with Danny.

Yes, yes. Yes! Danny was mad and let me know. I wish I could say this was the end of the insult that I imposed upon Danny that day. It wasn't. We exchanged words of anger and heartfelt condolences and then proceeded down Old Fort Bayou. Of course, we were charging away at full gallop of our pony-driven mobiles. I decided to overtake him on a two-lane road barely big enough for one lane. I came around him and inched my way past. I began to ease my way into the correct lane. Keep in mind that I am no driver, fellers.

I over under-estimated the distance between us by exactly two bumpers, his and mine. My bumper caught his and managed to bend both. I barely noticed it. He didn't miss it at all. We proceeded to Dead City, where he let loose all his anger. There was quite a bit of fear too since we knew our paps was going to kill us. Danny just yelled at me and called me a bunch of clearly correct adjectives. We both lived from the parental killings that took place that evening. Since this episode, Danny has always driven everywhere we have gone together, and that is no joke.

Don't go thinking that it is all Danny who had to put up with some heartache in this friendship. No, fellers. Danny has bent my metaphorical bumper a time or two as well. My first girlfriend was Tony. She was great. Five foot eight, blue eyes and blonde hair. Skinny like Olive Oyle. Mean like Brutus. Geesh, I loved that girl. I remember what she smelled like as she blow-dried her hair. The smell of her perfume, rightly named Poison.

Tony taught me to French kiss. I can remember that like it was five seconds ago. We were outside and it was slightly chilly. I was actually walking her home from Pete's house since she lived next door to him during school breaks. We had been doing the pecks on the cheeks for a few days when saying goodbye. Tonight, though, she sprung the question no feller likes to say no to. "Do you know how to French, Mark?" "Oui, oui!" I replied. It was a lie. I didn't even know what she was talking about. So much for that stupid book Pops gave me.

She came in close and pressed her lips to mine. I was like, *OK, I can handle this.* Then boom ba da bang she flicked her tongue out into my pursed lips. What could I do? I riveted back towards the side of the house striking my head on the bricks.

"I thought you knew how to French!" Tony said, surprised. "Oui," I said sheepishly. She followed up with some basic instruction. When we kiss, slightly open your mouth, and stick out your tongue to touch mine. I said OK. Once our tongues touch just move them about slowly. *Mmmm, this definitely was not in any book I have read.*

Dang it, I tried, and I liked it I tell y'all. This mouth tongue and all was funner than frog giggin on a Tuesday. I wanted to do this all the time with her. Poor ole Jaclyn Smith has been replaced. No, not Anne Marie yet, but it was getting close. Tony and I were well into our three- or four-day affair. I wanted to take her some place special to celebrate and get some more of that Frenching action. It made me feel so … well, it's hard to describe, but I liked it. I took her to the dirt hills. As we walked the path to the special path, Tony was particularly quiet. I am not much of a talker either so I just imagined what it would be like sitting on the hill and making Frenches with her.

Once we got there, we found a place to sit. I leaned in to begin the preplanned tongue exchange when she dodged me. SHE DODGED me, fellers and fellets. Oh, I had no idea what this was to be, but I knew twernt no good a-coming. "Mark, you and Danny are best friends, right?" I proudly responded with a positive. "Well, Mark, do you think you could get me his phone number?" Say what, how could this be? Apparently, it was his green eyes and nice lips. I was like, *I don't even think he has eyes or lips.*

I did not hesitate to give her my dearest ole pal's number though. The worst thing that could happen is that ole Danny boy would tell her how fantastic a feller I was, despite being small. Tony would realize he was correct and fall hopelessly in love with me. Fellers, you will understand this way more than fellets. There is a code that I was apparently unaware of. A feller gives up all rights to any fellet the moment she deems the original feller not worthy of her company, whether implicitly or obviously stated.

Ole Danny boy hooked up with Tony and although it lasted only moments in the span of a lifetime, it was a crusher. She did come back to me several more times. She was a free spirit and needed to find her place in life. I am the type of feller that, well I am just easy to leave and harder to come to. I accept that. I am not easy to figure out. I am after all a true-blue, heart-shaped, southern born and bred feller.

Danny and Pete have been my two closest friends since a young age. I am over fifty now and we are still hanging in there as friends. They are southern born and bred too. I guess that is why we understand the importance of friendship and loyalty. Without hesitation, we are there for each other. I could not think of a better blessing than that of a friendship of this magnitude.

As I close out this book, I don't want you to think these are all the events, or even details, I remember. It is just a small percentage of my memories. At this point in my life, I can still remember a lot of things. I remember wearing cloth diapers for instance, wait that may have been last week and it was Depends. Really though, I do remember wearing cloth diapers and crying to get out of the crib. I remember walking to the barbershop with my sisters and Grandpa Manieri. They had a pharmacy that had Barq's crème soda and candied sticks there as well. Root beer was my favorite.

I remember what it felt like to lay my head on Sambo, my dog, on a hot summer day. His heavy breaths would lull me to sleep in the middle of the woods or field. I can remember the day he collapsed coming in from playing with me. Later the same day, he was put to sleep, and we drove to Nebraska for my great-grandpa's funeral. I was sad to see my Grandpa Mark sad and sad about Sambo. That dog and I shared so much.

When the rain hits the hot asphalt, I remember so much time spent playing out in the street with all the peeps from the block. We didn't stop for rain or cold. Only thunder and lightning. Cold days remind me of hunting with my Uncle Joe. Sneaking through woods in search of something, not really knowing what I was doing. Later in life it was Danny and me hunting. I was hunting with Danny once, he in a tree stand far away from me, and I sleeping in mine. I had to poo (dern IBS). While in the act of pooing and weapon secured out of reach, two nice-sized bucks came strolling by well within reach. I could have caught them with a fishing pole, they were so close. They stared a moment, and I pooed a moment. I laughed as they wandered off.

I remember Anne walking down the aisle during communion and thinking to myself, *One day we'll do that together.* I remember the sting from the reality that the truth is she was never going to be anything to me than a first crush. Crazy enough, I remember watching *M.A.S.H.* and *Lawrence Welk* with my folks and then it was *Wheel of Fortune.* It took us a while to get cable.

I can remember times I was so scared that I couldn't move or cry or anything. My heart was beating so fast I thought I would die. My head was giving instructions and my body refused to commit. I was convinced the devil lived in my closet. I also remember walking through dark nights in the woods or spending the night out in my fort. I should have been afraid, but I wasn't. I was more at home than anywhere I have known.

The point is memories are important. I started writing this just as an attempt to salvage some of my memories. Time has a way of stealing so much from us. I have one photo album that is not even full. I have pictures of some folks I served with in the Navy. I have pictures of Drake and Sean, my nephews, one each. Danny and Pete. A picture of Tony and that is about all. If you were to look through my phone pictures it is mostly work-related photos, then my dogs, and then scenery. The rest of my memories are stored on this floppy disk inside this aging mind. So, when people ask me on the rare occasion, "Mark do you remember when …" I pause a moment for brevity and then I say, "Why yes, I remember when, I got arrested, I wrecked the car, I went 155 mph on a Katana, I met that gal in France, I saved a feller on Bourbon street, I swam over a mile, I skinny dipped in frigid temps, I roped a cow, birthed a baby, smoked a cigarette, I remember …"

WHAT DO YOU REMEMBER???

www.ingramcontent.com/pod-product-compliance
Lightning Source LLC
Chambersburg PA
CBHW020402130626
46549CB00006B/2406

* 9 7 9 8 9 8 9 5 6 3 2 0 3 *